Loving You Always

BETTY LOWREY

Copyright © 2019 by Betty Lowrey.

ISBN   Softcover   978-1-951469-85-6

All rights reserved. No part of this book may be reproduced or transmitted in any form or by any means, electronic or mechanical, including photocopying, recording, or by any information storage and retrieval system without express written permission from the author, except in the case of brief quotations embodied in critical reviews and certain other non-commercial uses permitted by copyright law.

Printed in the United States of America.

To order additional copies of this book, contact:
Bookwhip
1-855-339-3589
www.bookwhip.com

Nash's Journal

Perish Small Town, U.S.A. was not only about the adults who lived there, but a handful of girls that observed more than they would ever tell, heard things no one else wanted to hear and never forgot the important things. The problem was important to whom?

No one kept score of the missing people. The adults said, those reports that appeared through the year were mere fabrications. But when you are ten and eleven years old and you fear something might jump out of your closet at night, you begin to wonder are those stories true?

Remember, every adult was a child, even Jacob Long. He was once a famous baseball player, until he got hurt and lost everything. There was a mystery to him, all they knew was he walked the back roads, as if searching for something. What? And was it true, he was once Mrs. Delang's husband?

When Lily died they were sad and unsettled, not to mention scared and they felt they had to find who was responsible. It seemed the only person knowing how to comfort them was Mrs. Delang. Sometimes she just asks them to sit quietly and let their inner peace take hold while she played the piano. Lily used to sit beside her playing those songs; that's why I'll be loving you always, stuck in their minds.

Now the Pastor Of First Missionary Baptist Church has challenged his people to apply the love chapter 1 Corinthians 13:1-13 to their lives, every hour of the day he said, from the youngest to the oldest.

People missing, didn't anyone notice? Five girls investigating, a mother who recently lost her child, their friend, A Chief of Police who actually listens, but Nash overheard Mr. Troy Sanders telling his deputy, "I don't believe Jacob ever quit loving Charlotte, nor her him, and now according to the pastor, no matter what goes on in a small town, we are called to love everybody. But can you? As the story continues, where will it end? Like Mrs. Delang sitting at that piano playing, it just went on forever......

If I have not love
I am as a clanging cymbal
1 Corinthians chapter 13

Chapter 1

"The meeting will come to order." Nash beat her mother's wooden meat hammer against the makeshift podium, which in reality was an old desk top placed over a rusty barrel.

"Who made you the one to begin our meeting?" Audi demanded. Rising up from where she'd been sitting on a stack of old tarps, Audi crossed her arms and stood staring at Nash. "You in charge of us?"

"It's my home."

Audi glanced around, "Not hardly." She waited for the others to laugh. "This is your daddy's old shed. We need to clean this place."

"I don't think my daddy would like that. He likes everything out in the open so he can see it."

"Can you girls see everything?" Audi glanced around, enjoying their laughter.

"Sit down." Nash was hammering away, the meat hammer sounding mellow on the desk top. "We have important issues to discuss. Suzukki will read the preamble to our secret society."

"What exactly is a preamble," Audi inquired? "I'm lost on the rules you decided for us."

"A preamble," Nash replied standing and feeling important in her role. "A preamble states our purpose. It states why we formed our secret club and what we intend to do."

"Well, what do we intend to do?" Audi demanded. "I wasn't invited to help write the club's purpose."

There was a sharp rap of the meat hammer. Nash gave Audi a sizzling glance. "Sit down."

"You sit down. I intend to find out what this club I've joined is about. Stand up Bentley. You too, Galant, and don't act like you aren't interested. I heard you whispering back there."

"I'm thinking I don't want to be part of this secret club," Galant said. "I can't even say my chosen name without wondering what this is we've decided to do. When we said we would use the names of automobiles to disguise ourselves, cars that started with the same letter as our name, I didn't know G would turn up such words as gallant, gremlin, gembalia. Well, I thought Galant seemed regal and a leader…maybe I'll change if I can find something else."

Slowly, Bentley had risen to stand with her friends. "Our club was established to seek out the truth amongst teachers, preachers, older people and just about any age person that has a public problem. Like Mr. Tetner. He was blamed for having an affair with the Molly girl, fifteen years old, pretty and smart…way too smart for that ugly old wart hog that never brushed his teeth and his hair was oily. Ugh." Bentley gave a gagging sound. "If you believe that story, then you think I can fly, don't you?"

"That was unkind but true," Nash said from the Podium, her meat hammer in mid air. "We are tired of people claiming this and that and saying things untrue. We plan to root it out and publish in our secret magazine."

"So we all decided instead of using our own names we would take the name of an automobile. Man we had no idea how limited that would be… but we'd give our word and sworn the oath." Bentley glanced quickly to each one, "You do remember the oath? We were supposed to begin with the oath. I will be true to the ideals of the club we have created, to root out the meanness of the world where truth should reign and those who go against it burn in hell."

The meat hammer was pounding away, with Nash's face as red as a beet. "Bentley James, we are not allowed to curse. Besides that, those words certainly are not in our preamble…constitution, maybe but, anyway, Sit down Bentley and we shall take a vote on what pressing matter we should attend to first. Before we do, I want to read an interesting bit of news I read in our neighboring community's paper that my Daddy receives. Sand County is listed as a county where people go missing and are never found. Well, it listed names and I searched out those names."

"Can you guess what the majority of those names come up under? Majority means most, Audi?" No one guessed. "They ended up at Long's Funeral Service. Dead. Now, the Long's do have a Funeral home in different locations, so it could be that never comes to people's attention. But don't you think it's strange I'd run across that type of information? Who knows, our club might be instrumental in something just as important. Instrumental, Audi, means helpful. We might run on to something no one else would. The floor is now open for discussion."

Galant chewed nervously on her bottom lip. "Are any of you kin to that young couple with the new baby that lives on Waywood Street?" There was a general shaking of heads. "Then I think we need to investigate. He is leaving the house late every night. Like midnight and she stands in the window and watches him go."

"How do you know this?" Audi snapped the question before them all. "Midnight? Why are you up? Do you live near them to see this happening… remember, we are not to carry tales. It's our job according to the preamble to put out fires." She leaned back, importantly. "Right, girls?"

"All right then, we will all be on guard watching the young couple to see what he is doing. What a sadness….and them having a small child." Nash had done her best to lead the club today. "The first meeting of our club is dismissed. Now go out into the world and do good." She heard that on a radio program. "And on second thought," she said, "remember, we are all supposed to be living the love chapter this month. Pastor said so."

* * *

They arrived as agreed upon, one o'clock. Galant came huffing along, followed by Audi. "I tell you one thing I can't watch all of that daytime romance series and get here on time. Do you think we could meet fifteen minutes later? Right now, Bob Hughes has asked Lisa to marry him but his mother is upset about it." She glanced around to see what they thought. "I tell you it's a heartbreaker if they don't marry."

"Not me." Audi arrived in time to hear the question. "I have morning lessons, and then lunch and I just don't want to change it. Don't we need time to play? Besides, those are really old re-runs."

"Well, I'll ask the other girls. And another thing, my name is hard to say, I'm adding an i to the end of it. Galanti. Don't that sound better?"

"Not really, " Audi replied. "It's like I'd say, call me Audri. See? I added one little ole letter."

"You're just mad," Galanti replied. "It's kind of silly to choose the name of a car, anyway, Audri." She felt her friend tense up and saw the clenched fists too. Galanti smiled.

Nash and Suzuki arrived together. "I bet you girls hadn't thought of meeting over there in the shade of that big old oak had you? As president of this committee or maybe I should say club I motion we meet there, under the oak in the shade. All in favor say, aye." Four ayes followed.

"My mother said, "where you going, honey?" I said, we done formed a club and we named ourselves after cars so no one knows who we are. "Who are you?" She asked. "I'm Suzuki."

"What did she say, then?" Galanti asked.

She laughed and said, "Honey, just have your friends call you Suz, so they'll remember who you are. So how do you feel about that? I think she's right. From now on, I'm Suz."

"Well I'm sticking with Nash, nobody knows whether that's a boy or girl name and it just may come in handy. Now, let's get down to business. I inquired as to that young couple. It's okay. He goes to work around midnight and she is just sad he's leaving her alone with that baby."

"I done changed my name," Galanti replied, "and Audi here, I think she looks like an Audri, don't you?"

"I declare, Galant, follow the procedure, here, we've passed the name subject. We're on the young couple now. All in favor of discontinuing investigating them further, say I. Maybe that's aye."

"So, what's our next subject?" Galanti asked. "I vote we discuss our future. You know, when we grow up."

"You mean when we marry?" Audi cupped her mouth just so and said, "Ooooh. I prefer to discuss first we get out of grade school. Maybe then I can twirl that baton without hitting myself on the head. Those spinners in the air are real complicated for me. But I'm coming along on the piano. They're going to let me play Amazing Grace, next Sunday during worship service."

"I'm learning to cook," Bentley said. "Got no problem with the baton, but those cheers we're practicing seem abit awkward. I was supposed to do the flip last game, well you know what happened. It was embarrassing. Colley was the one nearest me, he said, "What's up, Bentley. Oh, it wasn't you, was it?" I felt like socking him, instead I said, "Hey, Colley, did you forget to throw the ball through the hoop, I noticed it kept hitting the wall behind, not once did it go through. You need to work on that."

They all laughed. "We're friends forever," they chorused, sticking up a pinkie until they formed a pinkie circle. "We got to watch this hurting each other's feelings," Audi said, "Or, we won't make it to our eight grade graduation as best friends and that love chapter won't mean a thing."

They paused to think on Audi's remark and then Bentley reminded, "We need to choose someone we can help before next week's meeting."

"On the way here, I noticed little Miss Salyer's got a lot of weeds around that tree out by the sidewalk," Suz smiled at the thought of kindness, "why don't we sneak in there after dark and pull all those little bugars and she'll wonder who helped her."

"Before we officially close the meeting of this club," said Nash, "let us make a motion to help sweet little ol Miss Salyer. "All in favor say aye." Five ayes were heard under the old oak tree.

> Though I have the gift of prophecy,
> and understand all mysteries....

Chapter 2

It was at the end of the week when the five mothers came together during the missionary society meeting.

"Mercy, what's next? Now our girls have this secret society and they've chosen secret names."

All the mother's enjoyed a laugh about the names. "Cars, mind You," Audi's mother said. "But then I guess it could have been worse."

"What's worse is their endeavor to help others" Suz's mother got their attention. "Someone pulled the blades right off little Miss Salyer's Day Lily's, stripped those blades right off the plant. It just rings of our girls."

"Why would you suspect them?" Galanti's mother ask.

"Well, I saw our girls inspecting them but from where else would Suz bring home a pocket full of green blades. I don't have any Day Lilies."

"Did you ask?"

"Of course I did and she says those old grass stems were long, Momma and we were just helping out a poor old woman that can't stoop and bend. It's a secret." So Suz Mother said, I decided just this once I'd keep their secret but we gotta keep an eye on our girls. They're hummin."

* * *

Summer wore on, the girls meeting at Lily Jane's Mother's home. Lily Jane didn't have a daddy. Someone said her daddy died in the war. The girls didn't ask which war that was. War meant a man was honorable and he served his country. Others said her daddy worked for the president and what he did was hush hush, so in Perish no one ask what that meant. Lily Jane's mother moved back to live near her elderly parents. It was a good thing those parents were well off, everyone said.

"What does well off mean?" Suz asked her mother. "Does it mean you got more money than most people?"

"Something like that. Why are you asking?"

"Well, Lily is not part of our group, but since she moved back and we all attend church together, we have been thinking, especially since she has a swimming pool in her back yard and ask us over, well…we have been thinking maybe we could ask her to join our group. Of course, then we could even have our meetings on days we're at her house in that nice cool pool. You know it has a pump that circulates the water and helps keep it clean?"

"No, I haven't been to that house in years. Now that her parents are elderly, I do know the daddy died. Mr. Granger, now he was a fine old man and his wife was generous and giving. Why sometimes she carried the women's missionary society when we sent all those medical supplies to foreign countries that had no idea what a band aid was and we'd send white strips of cloth. You can just imagine their delight in that cloth."

"Does Lily's momma fit in with you all?" Suz asked. 'You know it was Bentley said, "I think we should be nice to Lily. She can't help if her daddy died and she is practically an orphan. She needs a friend and I do believe that is part of our preamble isn't it? Or is that in our constitution to be nice to other people. Well, we took her in and what does she do, invites us to her pool. You can't lose being nice, now can you?"

It looked like everything was going well and then one day when the five were on their way to the First Missionary Baptist Church to make plans for Summer Camp. Walking along on that hot asphalt road, they heard the siren wailing in the distance. The Police Car lights were blinking and the driver was bumpin' down that country road coming toward them standing their looking at it.

"Get out of the road," Audi cried, "I don't think he sees us. Why he could run right over us." The girls spilled onto the grassy ditch, leaving the driver as much space as he needed. They craned their necks and watched as it pulled into Lily's drive. Their feet were stuck to the spot where they had stopped.

It wasn't five minutes passed; they saw the Policeman go to the door. He knocked and Lily's momma came to the door. It was three blocks away just a straight shot from the church to Lily's house but they heard Lily's

Momma scream. That scream pierced the air and air waves seemed to vibrate all around them. Doors opened on the street and they saw women stooped low peering out of screened windows.

Suz and Audi's momma's popped out their respective doors, located where the scream was coming from and headed toward Lily's house. The girls forgot the meeting they were to attend concerning camp and took off behind the mothers.

"No girls, you must turn back. We will let you know what's wrong. It sounds bad but we're hoping it's not. You go onto church and wait there. In time, we will come and talk to you. Mind now. Go back."

They sat for an hour listening to Miss Connie Poole describe the delights of Camp McMillen, named for the director of Missions in the Southern county, an affiliate with thirteen country churches operating beneath its banner. "They'll all be there," Miss Connie said in her glorious voice, "What fun we will have learning about Jesus and memorizing scripture."

"Will we swim in that same dirty old ditch as last year, " Bentley asked.

"Why, yes we will, Bently, a little mud and dirt never hurt anyone did it. It's caused by God Almighty's spring rains and aren't we blessed, living in agricultural area where our farmer's crops depend on rain?"

The girls suffered a few painful looks at each other remembering how hard that muddy water was to wash out of their hair under that one little downward faucet that some daddy had thought to string up on the outside of their cabin where water then ran along the yard with no other place to go and their shoes were caked with mud too.

"I wish I knew what was wrong," Nash whispered. "I think it's serious or it wouldn't take so long"

The church doors opened quietly and the girl's mothers stepped inside followed by their daddy's. The girls didn't move, didn't run to their parents. They knew something bad had happened. Their mother's eyes were red from crying. Miss Connie Poole asked, "Can you give us a word. We've been waiting."

Bentley's daddy crossed to where the girls sat. He stooped down, his weight on the heels of his feet as he was on their level, looking into each face before he spoke. "Your little friend has died. I was told Lily was hit by a car by someone that didn't even stop and check on her. Someone else came along and laid her on that old bench out by the highway. She has gone on to heaven to be with her daddy."

* * *

There was a meeting at Town Hall that night. Town Hall was an abandoned grocery store. The owner died and no one wanted to repair the many structural problems of the building but when a new set of government officials took place in Washington, suddenly there was mention of grants and Miss Alene Shelby sat down and wrote a pleading letter stating the small town needs of Perish and the town received enough money by doing the work themselves to make a fairly presentable Town Hall where it was said on occasion friends of the Creative Playhouse in the much larger town down the road might come in and perform.

You would have thought Miss Alene Shelby wrote Murphy's Law or something just as important to one's livelihood. She was touted as the woman of the year, honored with a gold trophy of a woman swinging a gold club because that was the only trophy the search committee found and she said it was fine because she intended to take up golf, anyway; just as soon as the next town over finished its golf course.

There they were, the five girls of the secret club, hiding out from their parents, all were wearing pajamas beneath loose fitting jeans. "We better spray heavy to keep the mosquitoes off or we will resemble Billy Colton when he had the measles and scratched til they covered his face."

The girls giggled and were properly shushed by Nash. "You'd think the mosquitoes own this old pine. They are flat buzzin,' I can't stand it."

"Where are we going?" Audi had been unusually quiet but something about the awful tragedy of the whole thing had opened her mind to a stream of questions. "My Momma will bust my butt if she finds out I've been here but I want to know why Lily was on the other side of town and who do they think ran over her?"

"First question, if you look to the farthest end of the building you'll see that window is open and that window is right over the bandstand Miss Alene Shelby was able to talk her husband and another man or two to build for the Fourth of July Celebrations. I'm thinking we can hide behind that old bench the city administration as they call themselves sit on during that celebration. You got it?"

"How do you know all this stuff, Nash?"

"I heard my Momma and Daddy talking. Their hearts are just about broke. They liked Lily."

Suz realized her own home had been as quiet as a tomb, her parents had nothing to say, sadness was as thick as butter in their home. All she had heard was her daddy say, "to think that person left a child."

"Shhh, we're almost there, watch that your shoes don't make noise on the boards," Galanti whispered. "That's why I told you wear your tennis shoes. Pass the word along, now, be quiet, no sound at all."

"I had to wear flip-flops," Audi replied. "My Momma washed my tennies, I guess they're hangin' on the line." Turning her head she whispered back, "Get quiet, no sound at all."

There were a few clumps and one giggle, but more shushing sounds as they embarked on the band stand floor Miss Alene Shelby had built for their town. Now they slid in file behind the old bench that smelled dank and full of mold. "I got allergies," Audi whispered. "I can't stay here long."

"Audi," Nash hissed, "Be quiet. They are praying. Now everyone bow your heads."

"Lord God almighty," Reverend Townsend's voice rang across the ages, joining with countless other situation and times of travail. "Heavenly Father our hearts are heavy over the loss of life in this little one, Lily Jane. We ask thy tender mercies and care on her mother. This child was ripped from her life and Lord we cannot imagine her pain. Thy guidance we pray on the one who did this, that this night repentance will come and a need to confess to the terrible deed of leaving this little girl alone on the roadside. We cannot fathom the endless heartache it has brought to this mother nor to the one who did the deed, leaving Lily Jane there on the side of the road. Give us understanding Lord, where it seems there is none. Give us caring and help us to leave judgement in your hands." They heard sobbing.

"I don't understand any of this," Audi cried. Real tears ran down her cheeks. "I ask momma to help me."

"Darlin," she said, "we don't understand either. Some things are in the Lord's hands and we won't know the answer until we get to heaven and he tells us. By then it won't matter as much anyway because we will see Lily Jane and everything will be made right."

"My Momma tried to explain its kind of like that second part of the love chapter," Suz offered. "We can't really see it, its dark like a shadow which is the mystery part, but someday we will either see it or understand it, I don't know." She sighed. "That love chapter is more than I want to learn. So, don't ask me about that prophecy part…that makes no sense to me, at all."

* * *

On Sunday, Audi hurried into the church building to find a bulletin saying she would be playing Amazing Grace during worship hour. But someone had forgotten, instead the words read as follows. Due to the death of our beloved little Lily Jane, all planned activities for our worship hour have been rescheduled.

Visibly upset, Audi sought out the Pastor, handed him a list and returned to the outside. When each of the club members arrived she pulled them aside and explained. "We are Lily's friends. We cannot sit by and listen two full hours to Reverend Townsend extol her virtues. I have already told him, we are going to do something to honor our friend. He just looked at me and nodded. You know as well as I do, kids our age don't have enough virtues for him to talk fifteen minutes. I'm going to play Amazing Grace. Bently what are you planning to do?"

"Well, in one of our meetings you mentioned twirling the baton is difficult for you. I'm pretty good at it, so I'll do that for Lily Jane. But I will have to run home to get my costume." So it went, on down the line, Lily's newly adopted friends prepared to honor her. "I'll sing a song for her," Suz said. "I wrote it last night so I don't have any music to go with it." Galenti sat there chewing her under lip. "I guess after we went home we all thought about Lily, didn't we? I wrote a poem. That's all I have. That leaves you, Nash."

"Yeah, well, I wondered how we could help everyone to remember. I'm not really good at it, yet, but I want to design jewelry someday. I'll have to have a second job because it takes a long time to be a good journalist. Last night I made about fifty bracelets. The middle stone is so small all I could do was put her name there, and then thread the little leather string through and tie it off. I have one."

Audi asked, "how in the world did you print those letters so small Nash? What a good job."

"I didn't, I have sheets of names or items and it was seeing the one with her name made me think to do this. You think I can give one to each person present?"

"You won't have enough. Skip up to third grade. We can go out and find some nice smooth stones to give to the young ones that didn't go to the back due to their own noisiness."

* * *

The girls were performing at their best and then it was time for Galenti's Poem.

"When I first met Lily I thought she's pretty enough, say's thank you a lot, and yes mam and yes sir too much But what if I don't like her? Then I heard her call my name she wore a smile on her face and she held out her hand for friendship's first touch and I liked her. Now she's gone, like the wind on a song and I haven't known Lily very long but I still like her. Lily, we are still friends, friendship doesn't end when one person goes away…in time we pick up where we left off, it's just another day."

Pastor Townsend stepped forward. "According to the list Audi gave me, we have one more."

Suz stood. "I don't have the lyrics put to music yet. I just wrote this last night while I was thinking about Lily. We had just met her and her mother and then she leaves us. Mrs. Marley," she glanced toward the piano, "it won't hurt my feelings if you want to play or if everyone wants to stand and sing. "I think the song would sound similar to You Lift Me Up."

Her voice sweet and soft, Suz began. "Jesus said, there is no love that we can know better…than to love a friend as our self. We share his love and friendship wherever we are, he is the light and we are the star. Our reflection picks up from Jesus, we cannot go this road alone…He gives us strength when we are imperfect, He is our friend and brings us eternal hope. He is the light….we are the star…he is the path that leads us to tomorrow…He is our hope, holding our place eternal…He is or friend and blessed us with you. We sing this song…in memory of Lily. We sing this song to honor you when we are old and meet our gift eternal…we will see you…Jesus words promise Where He is …there, we shall be also. Rest in peace, Lily. Jesus is the light you are the star.…"

Mrs. Marly accompanied Suz and everyone stood to sing with her. It was a most emotional moment. Every person understood the words, Jesus is the light, Lily, you are the star."

Pastor Townsend cleared his throat, "I believe our girls have captured words our own hearts have experienced. You are so right, Suz, without Jesus we would have no reflection, but with the light of his love we can be a star. As we close today, let us remember Lily's mother, she has lost her husband in service and now her child. May God's love be extended through a loving community. There will be a graveside service tomorrow, Monday morning at ten o'clock. God bless each of you as you leave God's house today."

Throughout the service, Troy, Perish Chief of Police had stood at the back of the auditorium observing everyone. Several seats were empty and he wondered to whom those seats belonged.

* * *

As was his duty, Aram Townsend knocked on the door. It was his task to do the final chapter of Lily's life. "I've come to discuss your plans for Lily's service," he said. "I'm honored you would ask me."

"I believe, Pastor, a memorial has already been done for my Lily, yesterday during your church service by those precious girls. At the cemetery, would you please read Audi's poem and perhaps those present would be so kind as to sing Suz's song because she is right, Lily was our star. She walked in the reflection of God's love. I don't know how we will travel through this new trial we've received. Right now, it is heavy on us. Tomorrow, I don't know what we will think or how we will handle it or each day that follows. Right now, I can only bury my child and wonder why this has happened."

Pastor Townsend glanced at the paper Lily's mother had given him. "You are in agreement with John's reading?" His troubled eyes met hers. "And a prayer will conclude the service for Lily?" She nodded. "I will leave you now," he said, "If there's anything you need, please do not hesitate to call."

"You may conclude as you are lead, Pastor," she said in parting. "The love passage is nice." He nodded.

He was in deep thought. Of course, Lily's mother would be upset, unsettled. She had lost a child but worse was the fact now in life she was alone, except for her elderly mother. Something seemed off-key, not just the fact of grieving. He couldn't put his finger on the problem but within himself he felt the depth of despair and his heart ached. All he could do was take it to the Lord.

Ten o'clock on Monday a subdued group walked quietly from the church building to stand by the open grave where Lily's casket would be placed. The five friends were ushered to the front by Long's Funeral Service. There were only two chairs, one for Lily's mother and the other for her grandmother. It was by special request the five friends would stand behind the two and they had been properly reminded by their parents not to whisper but to give undivided attention to the Pastor. If the parents were concerned the girls would not heed their advice, they need not worry; they were a solemn nervous assortment of emotional turmoil. This day would be embedded in their minds for the rest of their life.

Toombs could have been written had each person present's thoughts been recorded. A child? In all, if good was to come from wrongful happenings, what in the name of Jesus could be good about this? What purpose was man that they were born only to die? That point of view came from one who did not darken the door to Pastor Townsend's church. How do you go on having lost your child, the mother's wondered? The father's watchful eye moved around the crowd. Was he here, or was she here, the one who had done this? In their hearts the father's longed to fix this, but their hands were tied, no one had come forward, no one knew…but they did not buy into that story. Someone saw, someone knew. Long's Funeral Director glanced at his watch. There was a two o'clock for the chapel. Visitation for the ninety year old man would be starting about now. Ten years old versus ninety, who could wrap their mind around that?

Jacob Long was not one of the owners of Long's Funeral Home; he was a down on his luck distant cousin that ask for a job. "We don't have need for anyone right now," his Uncle said, while Uncle's Oscar's son, Raymond stood within hearing. "You're not trained for this type work, anyway." There had always been animosity between the two, since Raymond's daddy finagled the small farm out of the hands of their one living grandparent and that left Jacob's family on the outside looking in. It hadn't always been that way, once Jacob was a star athlete, he had gone from Perish thriving community to a baseball camp in Florida, and was picked to play ball for one of the winning teams of the day, but when Jack Harper's time came to bat he drove a hit right into Jacob's temple that knocked him to the ground and he hadn't been the same since. Some said it was the steel plate the doctors placed in his forehead trying to hold the inside and outside together, but Jacob knew that ball had nearly knocked the brain out of his head and truth was he had difficulty stringing two words together some days.

Today was not that day, when Uncle Oscar said to Raymond, "Little Lily's mother has requested white doves released as Lily's casket is lowered to the grave and her favorite song is played. We will have to take the battery powered box to play the song and you will be in charge of the doves."

"I'm not taking care of those nasty birds," Raymond said, all sullen and pouty for a thirty two year old man.

"I'll do it" Jacob said. "Uncle Oscar I'll take care of the doves. Do you want me to purchase them, too?"

> Though I have all faith, so that I could remove mountains, but have not love, I am nothing...

Chapter 3

The five stood as patiently as possible behind Mrs. Delang and her mother, Mrs. Granger. The white doves were a nice distraction but they did seem busy messing up the floor of the cage that held them. The man in charge of the doves seemed a nervous sort, but then he did have an important job. The birds. He seemed sad over Lily laying there in her white dress in the casket, like he knew her.

Pastor Townsend read from Ecclesiastes 3 and then he read the Love passage from Corinthians thirteen.

To everything there is a season and a time to every purpose under the heaven; a time to be born and a time to die; a time to plant and a time to pluck up that which is planted, a time to weep and a time to laugh a time to mourn and a time to dance….. Audi wondered if Lily could hear the words. She looked like she could, and she would have liked the doves, Audi just knew she would. It was time for the dove release. Somewhere over the rainbow blue birds fly, birds fly over the rainbow…

"Those girls," people would say many times through the years as they told the story, "Those girls stood as brave and strong as a soldier, but when that song began you could see each one swallow as a tear ran down cheeks. There was something about seeing those white birds fly up into that bright blue sky and hear Judy Garland sing somewhere over the rainbow blue birds fly….."

Everyone knew they longed to stand by their parent and have those comforting arms hold them close, but they stood there with Lily's mother and when it was over they kissed her cheek and told her they would miss Lily. Mrs. Delang hugged them, so tight they felt her sadness press through their body. Then she kissed Lily's cheek one last time and Pastor read the love passage as Lily's casket was closed.

Her hand on the casket, "Girls," Those nearby heard her whisper, "don't forget me I'll be waiting for you this Thursday for the weekly meeting. Yes, I'll be there by the pool. Don't forget me."

* * *

Perish had become a town that didn't know what to do with its self. After Lily's gravesite rites, in respect the people moved on. Many desired to visit graves of loved ones but it seemed inappropriate. Mrs. Delang and her mother needed a moment alone with Lily before leaving the cemetery.

The usual dinner prepared by ladies of the First Missionary Church was dismissed due to Mrs. Delang request. "What would we do but drown in our own sorrow? There's just Mother and me. We have no relatives." For a moment a cloud came across Charlotte Delang's expression but she chose not to share.

"But you have us," Suz mother comforted. "I know it's not the same but we won't let you suffer alone."

Charlotte Delang touched her friend's hand. "I know Carol Lynn, you have the kindest intention and loving heart but I cannot do this. I must take mother home and we will somehow get through this day."

* * *

"What will we do?" Audi asked the group standing against the church building, observing those who had come to mourn Lily's passing. The five whispered among themselves. "We have to cover every street of this town," Nash said, "I believe if we watch the people and listen to their strange conversations we may find clues to what happened to our Lily." Bentley's own thoughts were in line with Nash. "But our window of opportunity is slowly fading." Audi was captured by those words, "What in heaven's name does that mean?" Bentley whispered, "I heard that on the news, it means we don't have much time."

"Do you think Lily's Mom wants us to come to her pool for our meetings?" Audi asked. "I'm not sure we can have a meeting and discuss that we are looking for the person who…you know…"

"Who killed Lily," Nash explained. "We will have to discuss something new each week that has nothing to do with our investigation." Audi gave Nash a puzzled look. "It means we are searching. I heard that on the news, too." Nash and Bently nodded.

"I'm not allowed to listen to the news this week," Audi confided. "I don't sleep well. So I can't listen."

Suz was listening. Without adding to the conversation she reached for Audi's hand. "I'm having trouble, too."

"Before we go to Mrs. Delang's on Thursday, we will meet here unless it's raining, then we don't have to." Nash was resuming her rightfully appointed position as leader of the group. "Wear your swimming suits but don't let them show just in case Mrs. Delang didn't really mean to invite us."

"Then why would she?" Audi demanded. "She told us to come and not to forget her."

"Grief," Nash replied, solemnly shaking her head. "My mother says often in grief things are said that a person didn't mean to say. All we can do is show up Thursday to see if she is sitting by her pool."

"We have three days to case this town," Suz added. "I think we should go home and change clothes and begin." Audi was wearing that puzzled expression again. "Case means investigate, that's what we'll do."

"My Daddy," Bentley began, "said sometimes it takes years to find out the real truth why something happened and in a small town, people don't talk and when there's foul play there's always someone trying to cover it up. I guess that's our clue, to find someone acting suspicious, covering up something."

* * *

Sheriff of the County Wade Bradford had called a special meeting with a select group of men from the town of Perish. Population two thousand one, Perish was one of the more thriving towns under his supervision of Sand County. It was the school kept the town from going under. Lose your school, the shops closed up with store fronts empty and parking spots bare. Keep it and there was commerce.

The father's of the girls he'd seen standing behind Mrs. Delang were present. The city police had rebelled that he was opening the meeting. "It's our town," they declared. But Wade Bradford was having none of that. "I was duly elected Sheriff of this county, boys, and I don't take that calling lightly. A precious little girl's life has been taken and I want to know who's responsible. What information have you collected?"

There was a bit of shuffling of feet. When the volunteer Police Force hesitated, Jared Stiles stepped forward. "Sheriff, I'm father of one of the girl's you saw standing behind Mrs. Delang's chair, and I'm mayor of Perish. You know me and I think our Police Force is hesitating to answer your question because our little city has nothing, nothing to answer your question."

"Who found the girl's body?" The Sheriff asked. "I read the account in your newspaper and of course the statistics came in to our office but the article didn't have a blame thing on who is suspect. I know, I know you can't name names but was there someone you suspected, have brought in, are watching?"

Red faced, Troy Sanders, Perish own chief of police stood. "You come in here, take over our meeting, ask your questions and seem to talk down to us. The truth of the matter is, the crime scene was clean. I'm wondering if the body was transported. We don't know why Lily Delang would be on the other side of town. We asked Mrs. Delang and she was distraught. She said they put Lily in her own bed the night before."

He glanced around the group. "We have nothing because we can't fabricate something that wasn't there. What we are doing is scouting the town; there'll be not one nook or cranny escapes our attention. Now unless you have information, I suggest this meeting adjourn because we have jobs to do. As your news commentator said so aptly. Our time of finding something that leads us to the killer has a short window, closing as we speak."

Reluctant, the Sheriff motioned his two men toward the door. "It's plain we aren't wanted, but I tell you Troy, we will be doing our work regardless of your stand on this situation. Lose one little girl, you could lose another. Slight one family you'll have an uprising. You're no different than me, our bread and butter rests on the shoulders of Sand County residents.

If we work together we get things done, otherwise we hamper the whole investigation." The mayor was following the sheriff out the door.

"We'll take care of our own," Troy Sanders replied.

The father's were taking in each word. Something didn't seem just right. They left, walking out to the Mayor's car. Jared stiles waited. "What's that about, Jared?" It was Galanti's dad asked the question. The mayor threw his hands up in the air.

"Beats me, Wish I knew."

The girls had positioned themselves beneath the window of the Police Station. At this hour the temperature remained hot and humid. They knew the window would be cracked so they could hear.

"It's time we go to work," Nash said. "We split up and canvass the neighborhoods. Audi, why are you wearing flip flops? You know with all this walking you should be wearing tennis shoes."

"You wear what you want, Nash. I'll take care of my feet." She glared at Nash. "You are not my boss."

"I don't want to hear you cryin' when your feet start hurtin." She stared at Audi's feet. "Those things are nothing but a thin piece of rubber, no support at all.'

"You're just repeating what your own Momma says, Nash, so shut up and leave me alone. You hear?"

"What's going on, Audi?" Bentley laid her arm around Audi's shoulders. "You still worried?"

"You heard what the Sheriff said, lose one little girl, you might lose another. Wasn't that his words?"

* * *

Chief of Police, Troy Sanders waited patiently for Charlotte Delang to answer the door. He had seen the pool and now he heard the lull of the motor, occasionally it seemed the motor hiccupped making a thin spray of water splash against the tiled walls. A kids floaty had lodged under one of the eaves, that small overhang that sheltered the holes necessary for circulating the water and if needed, drainage. No need for that float now, he was thinking.

"Troy." Charlotte opened the door, motioning him in and leading further into the screened porch. "Shall we sit out here or had you rather go inside?" She glanced up to the ceiling. "The fans provide a movement of air. I think we can be comfortable."

Troy was conscious moisture caused by the heat had left damp spots on his shirt. "You always look nice, Charlotte," he said. "Cool in the warmest of temperatures. We are in for it, I'm afraid; they forecast ninety degree weather this week." Charlotte only smiled. "We've known each other since first grade, haven't we but we lost track when you married and moved away." He sighed, glancing around. "This is nice. Your Momma and Daddy always led the community in their pristine way of keeping the property."

"Thank you, Troy. But with Daddy gone and Mom ailing, it has its spots of disarray, and needs repair."

He swallowed and cleared his throat. "You know I'm here about Lily. How did it happen, Charlotte?"

She gave him a sad glance and then lowered her head; her voice was barely a whisper. "I wish I knew. Did we do something to cause this? You raise your child thinking they'll outlast you, and then at ten years old you don't even have your child?" For a minute she raised her eyes to his. "My mind is in such a fog. I put her to bed expecting to see her the next morning but instead I receive a phone call from some stranger who says my child is laying on that old bench we all pass by that sits out on the highway."

That's where the Linc children's daddy tied it to a tree for them to sit on while they waited for the bus." Nervous, Troy cleared his throat again. "I know that part, Charlotte. It was early morning when first Jacob Long found her, but he didn't have any way of letting us know. Then he comes in town with Herm Johnson bringing a load of pigs to the sale barn and finds that one of my men received a call and his Uncle Oscar Long's Service had already left." He gave her an apologetic glance. "You already know this; we are going over everything, Charlotte, trying to piece this thing together."

"I appreciate your effort, Troy," Charlotte stared across the room. "It seems like a bad dream until I realize she's really gone." Her voice trailed off, "My baby. Our Lily." She made herself return to the moment. "I would never have thought anyone in Perish would hurt a child. I cannot comprehend this, Troy. It's unreal. I don't want to believe it. But if someone with an evil intent hurt my baby…" A tear dripped from the corner of her eye and ran down her cheek, scrubbed away as quickly as it came. "My mother is distraught. I know she's in the first stage of dementia, Troy, but this has confused her more. She wants to walk the field that lies behind the house, and I can't let her do that. What if she got lost?"

"I hate to ask at a time like this, Charlotte, but have you had any contact with Jacob?" He watched her cheeks flush with embarrassment. "It's just that his showing up at a time like this…even if it was before. I know your and his history, Charlotte and I questioned was it coincidence or part of a plan?"

"Plan, Troy? I don't think I'm following your meaning."

"You and Jacob were high school sweethearts, Charlotte, then he goes away to train for some high rigged ball team and you go off to college and word had it that you were pregnant. Some said it was a secret marriage that your parents didn't want. Speculation had him taking the child away from you and raising it by himself. He made good money at first but then the accident happened and slapped him down in more ways than one. Did he take the baby away from you, Charlotte?"

"Why would you say this? What gives you the right to question me or to dig up my personal records?"

"Am I the only one knows you had another child, Charlotte, a daughter that's what…eight or nine years old by now. I heard you turn down the church ladies dinner. You said you have no other family, just you and your mother. But I know that's not true. Does Carol Lynn know about your first child?"

"No." Sadness claimed her. "It was a secret wedding because my parents didn't like Jacob and thought he'd never make enough to support me. But it wasn't long until Jacob was rolling in the money, But he was never home. When we divorced he could hire the best lawyers. I got out by the skin of my teeth and with my daughter. But the courts gave her to him because he was financially set to see to her needs."

"What are you going to do if he tells it around town?"

"He won't. He promised." She wiped the flood of tears into her hairline. "I wanted my baby; I just couldn't deal with what Jacob's team members put me through. In those days Jacob had a good heart, but then he took my baby didn't he and I formed another opinion of him. I wasn't even allowed visiting privileges."

She wiped her hand on the bottom of her blouse. "She doesn't know me at all," she said bitterly. "It was as if I didn't exist. Money talks in certain places and especially if you know the right people. Lawyers, judges, government officials like to rub shoulders with proven athletes and back then, Jacob was stepping high. All I wanted was my daughter but how would that affect his reputation? I still want her but someone signed my name saying I would never make contact with her. I went to court and was laughed out of the courtroom. He's famous his lawyer said, who are you?" I wanted to scream, I'm Macie's mother. Did he give birth? Did he carry her in his belly? Does throwing a ball mean you can take away a mother's child. What he did to me.I..I have to pray daily for forgiveness because of my thoughts."

"You know he's not allowed to drive now, no license issued, some say he needs a guardian. What do you think?"

"I think he can rot in hell. If Macie ever wants to know about her mother, I'm here, but who will tell her."

"I hear he still has money but there's a board of people, maybe even those lawyers and judges you mentioned who are in control of it. Your ex-husband is not resting on his laurels, Charlotte. If anything he is a prisoner of his own making due to that metal plate they put in his head."

"I don't want to waste your time or mine, Troy, talking about him. Do you know....... where is my daughter?"

Troy shook his head and started walking away. "I'm truly sorry, Charlotte for this conversation. Please, forgive me. But there's one last thing you might find interesting, Raymond Long is trying to gain control of Jacob in order to control his wealth. "

* * *

Troy Sanders studied Jacob's record. His profile ended long before his cousin Raymond came on the scene hoping to secure custody of Jacob in order to have the money garnered when Jacob was at the top of his game. He had tried to speak to Oscar, but the old man warded him off, "I won't discuss my son with you, Troy, nor my nephew. I told Raymond to stop proceedings, but he 's right in one thing, someone better take care the boy or he's going to die out there on the road like poor little ole Lily."

"Then, you are justifying the end of the means, although you and I both know it's not Jacob's welfare your son is interested in but the financial gain he sees coming from it." He eyed the old man and saw the cunning look in his eye. "So you're in it, too, but you'll let your boy take the fall if it doesn't turn out according to plan, and if it goes completely wrong and there's blame, you'll say, "Raymond had his cousin's best interest at heart. He was trying to help him but you just can't help some people."

"That's about it," Oscar agreed. "You can't pass this on, now can you, Troy? You being duly elected and me, well, I have attended to most folks in the county's needs one time or another and I'd say I'm in good standing with them, but you now, someone could say something derogatory about you and ruin your chance at reelection, couldn't they?"

"If that's a threat, Oscar, I don't think your reputation is quite as sterling as your own opinion. Could be enough jewelry on dead corpse has gone missing that some cast a doubtful eye your way."

Oscar's face reddened. "You watch what you say, Boy. I could have you fired in a heartbeat."

"Oh, I'm aware of your bosom buddies, Oscar. I'm just sayin' the pot can't call the kettle black, and I've as many in my pocket as you. Except mine are younger, and yours, well yours have one foot in the grave."

"You are going to regret this conversation." Oscar's mouth was set in a grim line and his eyes glowed like coals of fire.

"You remind me of stories of the devil, incarnate, Oscar. There's even a smell about you. Maybe its that formaldehyde you use, I don't know but lest you try to push me out of my office, let me remind you, the case of Mrs. Goldsmith's diamond disappearing off her finger before the lid of the casket closed was a firm case against you. If you hadn't been in such a hurry to take those diamonds to Hargas Jewelers to have them reset for your wife, maybe I'd never have known…but you messed up not knowing Mrs. Goldsmith bought those diamond rings from Hargas Jewelers in the first place and Mr. Hargas recognized them."

The old man, for all his fuming and jerking body movements became still for a moment as he considered whether the Chief of Police was bluffing.

"That's right, Oscar, they didn't face you up because the siblings wanted the money from the insurance company instead of the diamonds. They'd already filed their claim and it was forthcoming. Hargas decided not to ruin you. You got a strange ally there, Oscar, but it doesn't mean he likes you."

Rising from his chair, Troy left the file on the desk. Evil hides in strange places, he thought and sometimes in those who smile the most. He'd known a number of morticians, good ones that truly shared the grief of families but this one…a dark thread ran through that family…maybe there was more to it than he knew. Still in his mind Raymond's motive was wrong. Troy needed something light to erase the feeling he'd received in remembering his and Oscar's conversation. He needed something sweet in his life to take away the meanness of people. He went outside.

Across the street stood Lily's five little friends. He crossed over. "Good morning, Girls. You girls on duty, or something?" They gave him puzzled stares. "I mean like Nancy Drew or Sherlock Homes, are you girls on assignment?" They were mute. "If you are helping with this investigation," he paused, "Consider every act you perform, don't go into dangerous places. Tell your parents who you are with and where you are going." Again, he paused. "I saw that look. No secrets here, "line up, single file, stand straight, yeah, that's better, now here are your orders. "First, your safety is of utmost importance, how can you help others if you don't take care of yourself. Last, remember to report back to me. That's all."

"How does he know what we are doing?" Audi was amazed and a bit fearful of men wearing uniforms.

"He doesn't," Nash affirmed. "He's bluffing." But she did wonder why he even stopped to talk with them. Her Daddy's words came to her now. "My Daddy says, That Troy Sanders is a good man but this investigation may be his undoing."

"What does that mean, his undoing?"

Nash studied Audi. "I don't know. Falling apart, maybe. I guess we'll have to wait and see."

* * *

Red faced, hot, their bodies trying to accommodate the heat of the day, they sat down under the large oak in the park. The shade was creeping away from the tree at the moment to the East. Several mothers were watching toddlers digging in the sand boxes that were new this year to the park.

"There's dog poop hidden in that sand. What're they gonna do when their baby comes smearin it on them?"

Audi met Suz's eyes. "Cat poop, too, ain't nothin' smells like that." She gagged at the thought. "When I grow up I ain't takin' my baby to the park."

"You're here," Nash reminded. She was going through the notes everyone had collected and turned in. "Bentley, what's this about a piece of material that reminded you of Lily's dress? I can't hardly read your writing. Does it say on the bumper, is that front or back and how large was the piece?"

"Oh, it was just a shred, kind of stuck in the crack next to a dent on the passenger side of the car."

"Why'd you think it worth listing?"

"Because," Bentley explained, "it looked like Lilly's dress." She lay back on the ground. No grass, just dirt where the Park attendants had scraped it clean.

"Your hairs goin to be nasty. Do you wash it every night?"

"Momma makes me." She threw her arms out thrashing as though she were in a snow storm making snow angels. "Where's Galanti, she's missed the last two meetings. Didn't we make a rule, miss three and you're out?"

"It might matter if your momma won't let you come. Galanti's mom says too much talk about Lily and we'll all have nightmares."

"She's got that right." Suzuki agreed. "Every night I go to bed I expect something to pop out of my closet or from under the bed. Momma and Daddy won't let me crawl in bed with them anymore. They say I got to grow up." She gave them an indignant snort. "All the years ahead and they want it now?"

"But Lily didn't get to grow up," Bentley reminded her.

"You still play with dolls?" Audi was curious, seemed to her sometimes they all wanted to act like teens. Right now they wouldn't answer the question, each one waiting on the other and no one willing to say. "I do," Audi informed them. "If I plan to be a momma some day, then it don't matter, its practice."

"What about you, Nash?" All eyes were on Nash. She ignored them. Her responsibility made the secret club a job rather than having fun. Today was work, tomorrow…"Well, tomorrow we are suppose to go to Mrs. Delangs. You all remembered, didn't you?"

"Do we have to?" Galanti don't know about it, does she? It's going to be awful sad. I vote no, don't go."

"We can't do that," Nash scolded. "We gave our word and we even kissed her cheek. We're going. In the afternoon. That water will feel so good. Meet here at one fifteen. Don't let your swimming suit show in case she forgets she asked us, we don't want to be rude."

"We better think about that," Audi replied. "If we can't get by with being rude now, we never will."

"I declare, Audi," Nash's face was red from exertion. "What is going on with you, you've been in a mood all day."

"Maybe I miss Lily," Audi retorted. "Maybe I don't sleep good and I'm worried about all the little girls in this town. Maybe you should be too, Miss high and mighty."

"I told my mother, you are so hard to get along with. You complain, you go against our plan. You're just hard to get along with and I'm wore out trying."

"You want to be my friend," Audi asked, "then get used to it. Life, as you tell us over and over and over is short and we better work out how we feel about it. Well, if I don't agree with something that's how I feel. Besides that I bet you play with dolls. If I were them I'd hate for you to be my momma."

Bentley saw Nash start to get up. "Don't do anything, Nash. She's the youngest of us. If Audi questions everything or doesn't understand, we used to be just like that. She doesn't mean to hurt your feelings she's just on overload. Losing Lily set off a lot of emotions in us. I feel kind of let down, myself."

Nash had got to her feet anyway and stood towering over Audi. "It's not my fault and I'm tired of you acting like this Audi."

Audi reached found a handful of loose dirt and threw it at Nash's feet. "Get used to it," she said. "I can't help it."

"You are a brat, just like my Momma says." Now both girls had tears in their eyes. Audi didn't tell anyone goodbye, she just headed home. "She's plain hateful and I can't stand it," Nash said.

"Or, like Mrs. Delang, distraught. Her neighbor, more than one neighbor, told my Mom, Mrs. Delang plays the piano night and day, as though to rid herself of deep dark terrible feelings. They can feel it, the piano pounds deep bass to the high end notes so full of sadness they feel it. Her main song is I'll be loving you always. Or, maybe the pastor's words to love everybody's hard for her after losing Lily." Bentley sighed, "You might want to think about that, Nash, Audi's younger and things use to bother us, too."

>   And though I bestow all my goods to feed the
>   poor and though I give my body to be burned
>   but have not love…it profits me nothing.…

Chapter 4

Charlotte finished with the calls to the girl's parents. "Mother," she explained, "It would not be right if I did not make the calls. I was afraid the parents might have misgivings about their child coming here, but they said no. They are fine people. Good parents." She sighed missing Lily. Her eyes filled with tears. She clutched her hands to her chest. "Oh, Mother, it hurts, right here. Such emptiness."

In one of her lucid moments Mrs. Granger replied. "I felt the same when your daddy died, dear." Then she sat down in the rocking chair she had moved to the kitchen and stared into space the next hour while Charlotte made cool aid, and placed cookies on a paper doily plate. It was when the clock chimed the half hour before one, Mrs. Granger said, "your father will be home soon, sweetheart. We should wash up for dinner."

* * *

"Girls." Charlotte met them poolside. "Are you wearing your suits? You look so proper." She hugged each one. "Is that our Audi straggling up the street? Did you run off and leave her?"

"No, ma'am," Nash replied. "Audi is in a bit of an emotional upheaval of late and we don't know what to do about it, so we leave her alone."

"Me, too," Charlotte said, glancing at the float that always reminded her of Lily. "I don't know what to do about it, either." She took her place in the one reclining chair and left the others for the girls. "Swim as you wish, girls and before you leave we will have the meeting. Today, I thought we'd talk about something simple. I have this feeling you all are at a loss… that's what we'll discuss, how to deal with loss. You can help me." She tried to smile brightly, but the smile dissolved into a sad face of despair. Audi arrived, not knowing what was expected of her. Opening her arms,

Charlotte provided the only thing Audi needed; acceptance. And soon, Audi was splashing with the others, her laughter pealing across the water to where Charlotte sat remembering.

* * *

Suz walked home with Audi. "Is it getting any better?" Audi didn't reply. "You know, the closet thing and under the bed?" She sighed, swinging her towel around like a lasso. "I'm down to a night light now. Do you think Mrs. Delang leaves a light on?" Suz leaned down to peer up into Audi's face. "Don't shut me out, Audi. I need you for my friend."

"My Momma called Nash's mother. She was mad that she told Nash I was a brat for saying how I feel."

"What did Nash's mother say to that?"

"That she was sorry. In the future she would refrain from her thoughts spilling out into words."

"Did it help?" Suz was trying to grasp the meaning of her friend's mother's words.

"No, my Momma hung up on her. She said, the nerve of that woman. So it wasn't good, was it?"

"Like we talked about loss; Mrs. Delang said we should all say one word that described loss. She began with the word empty. My word was missing, what was yours, Audi?"

"Gone."

* * *

The first weeks were awkward. One thing was settled; the girls asked their parents to let them miss camp. Being away nights might prove troublesome and what parent wanted to take a late night ride to bring their child home? The summer heat continued to beat down and the girls were happy to meet each Thursday at Charlotte Delang's swimming pool. "I wish your mother's would come with you," she said, one day as the girls were leaving. "I don't suppose that's possible, though."

Her voice held its usual wistfulness; sad enough the five remembered her words and told their mothers. The next week, Charlotte's wish came true. Each friend hugged her and said, "I didn't want to interfere, Charlotte. If you need me, I'll always be here for you. Why we go back to school days, don't we?"

There was an ease settled into the Thursday's they spent together. The tinkle of laughter gentle and soft grew into a healing of sorts. Now they embraced the hours, gentle hearts that held kindred thoughts, minds that explored the future. Perhaps in time the fears would be replaced, the boogie men of the dark hours erased.

Charlotte's pool was closed the week after school began. Around Perish crops were maturing and the first of harvest had begun. Mother's of the five resolved to continue the weekly visits. "We'll begin practice for the children's Christmas program, Charlotte," Carolyn Ann said, "Is it too soon; will you feel up to returning to church? We've missed you." The other mother's nodded. "It's not the same without you."

"I never meant for it to be this long," Charlotte replied. "But what will I do about Mother? Her body is stronger than her mind. If she decides, she breaks away from me." A sadness crept into Charlotte's voice, "That strong will she's had through life remains, it's the channel to control it is missing."

"We will be there to help, dear and our husbands, too. You come along we need you and hopefully you need us. We really don't always have someone to play the piano, and you do that wonderfully."

"The memories batter my mind," Lily's mother whispered. "Do you think I'm coming along, naturally? Or am I stuck in the fog?"

"It's the circumstance," one replied. "The complete silence that holds you in this stage of suffering is unreal. That no one knows how Lily was taken to that old bench just takes us down the road to nothingness. Why hasn't someone come forward? Our Police tried. The Sheriff says he has pursued his investigation and it won't be closed until something concrete comes along." She sighed, "you have held up, Charlotte and we keep you in our prayers that time will help you. We just don't know your pain."

They were in Bentley's home. Her mother paused. The fact her husband was Mayor of Perish should mean something, but it didn't. "God bless you, Charlotte. Perhaps time will give us the answers."

The mothers aim was to keep Thursday's gathering, a page from Charlottes book… continued healing for young minds who had lost part of their innocence in losing Lily. Now, there were eleven coming together and a bond of friendship had settled firmly in their midst. "My, these girls have turned into ladies," Charlotte murmur, looking on.

"And you had a hand in it," Bentley's mother replied. "What you did, taking an interest in them after losing your own, Charlotte what a blessing. We didn't know, we just played it by ear, but you knew their pain and through caring you brought them through. How many people would have taken the time?"

"How did you know what to do, Charlotte?" Suz mother had arrived late but was listening to the conversation now. "We had such a traumatic time dealing with Suz. She had never wet the bed, and then all of a sudden there were nights she would come into our room embarrassed and distraught because it happened. The doctor said the innocence of youth takes many turns in dealing with pain. The bed wetting ceased sometime after you began your Thursdays with the girls but how did you know their pain?"

"Through my own pain, Charlotte replied. It was something Jack would have done."

"We didn't know your husband. Tell us about him." The ladies settled around the table to listen.

"I met him through church. He was a lay leader, meaning he had not yet accepted pastor ship of a church and of course my being divorced, they frowned on our relationship. We married in secret, even going against Jack's principles. He was called. The Lord looks on his own, regardless of what the powers of the world see. In time, based on Jack's own merits and societies weakness…many divorced people in congregations are left to their self the church not knowing what to do with them and they flocked to Jack's ministry. He was a good man with a purpose to love others. It's not ours to judge, he would say in that powerful voice. Leave that to the Lord and get on with life. The scripture says love others."

"You do that very well," the mother's commented.

"In most cases, but you know my past. My history of Jacob…" she paused. "I have to pray for forgiveness there because we went through such a terrible time…it was before his injury that disrupted the high life style he had become accustomed to…" Her sigh was deep, "I have my own demons."

"What will you do, Charlotte, if you come upon him? He's here. Raymond Long, his own cousin is trying to gain custody of Jacob. Do you really think there's need of that? Or is Raymond seeking opportunity to take over the untouched wealth from days when Jacob was making a name for himself as the story goes because now Jacob is unable to take care of his own business?"

Charlotte listened when another said, "I hear Raymond is just waiting for the old man to die, but if he does who will pull Raymond out of the mess he gets himself into? I know for a fact he won't help and they've hired a new guy from some other town, that one said fired at his last job and down on his luck, I think his mother lives here, a Mrs. Dawsey. I can't imagine the Longs hiring someone off the street expecting people whose loved one has died to put their trust in the hands of some fellow off the street, not to mention their funeral service. I don't know her or her son but the story doesn't go well for Raymond or Oscar. Makes you wonder?"

"I haven't encountered either of them, but my memory of Raymond?" Charlotte shuddered. "He was different. The two were like oil and water. After Oscar won the court's approval, the farm was his and Jacob's family that watched over the grandmother and took care of the farm…well, they were told to leave and the bitterness of being shoved out of something they loved nearly killed them."

"Jacob had good parents?"

"The best. Before Oscar won the farm the proceeds were split but after Oscar the farm was solely his and the remainder of the family received nothing."

"I can tell you one thing, if Raymond gains custody, Jacob will be looking at the inside of an institution. What's the delay over the court date? I keep hearing it's changed again. I think Raymond is waiting for Jacob to mess up. You know, if Jacob does anything to cast doubt on his sanity, that's when Raymond will pounce. He makes me think of some big old vulture circling in the air."

"Those are fighting words, LeAnn." Nash's mother spoke her mind. Bentley's mother was prone to keep silent, after all her husband was Mayor but in Perish the title was more prestige than financial gain. "I think we would fall under Charlotte's husband's group," Mary said. "We're judging."

Charlotte listened. Jacob's turn in life did not make her happy. Jacob was her first love, fame had come so quickly a boy from humble background had no chance against the offerings the world gave to him. Parties in homes that cost more than the farm his parents worked. Women throwing their self at his feet, knowing he had a wife and child, but the odds were in their favor because the little wife was home with that child, simple, plain and devoted. But the devotion didn't last after she read the newspapers. In the beginning, Jacob said, "Honey, what am I to do? You choose to stay home with our child. Hire someone to take care of Macie and come with me." But she wouldn't entrust her child to another days on end, there were too many stories.

It was Jack said she must lose the bitterness toward Jacob. "He doesn't feel it," Jack would say, "but its eating you up. It's like poison." You didn't experience it, she'd reply and Jack would take her in his arms and hold her. Then one day Jack was gone; too soon, from a heart attack that ripped his heart apart. He was gone instantly. "For that, be thankful," the doctor said. "Jack would never have been the same. All that energy we remembered, would no longer frame the man."

Charlotte brought her attention back to the women discussing an incident that happened at church. "He sits quietly on the back row," Bentley's mother was saying. "You have to wonder what he's thinking. Lost everything, barred from places and still there beats a heart inside that body, God forgive us all."

She didn't ask who they referred to, in her mind she wondered was Jacob like that; A prisoner inside his mind, just as her mother? Who was caring for Macie, if he was in that shape? If it was his parents then there was no worry. No finer people walked the earth but her next thought was startling, they were getting older. A plan developed in her mind, there, as she sat in her friend's home. Macie, her mind whispered. Macie.

"Charlotte, our piano's a bit out of tune, but before we leave each other, why don't you play for us?"

"I'll be loving you, always," the ladies sang, arms around each other's waist, "With a heart that's true."

* * *

It was Saturday; the girls were sitting on the benches in front of Acorn, the store with style. "What exactly is Acorn about?" Audi realized she didn't pay much attention to what was in a building.

Nash waited, but no one replied. "It's a clothing store with a certain type clothes. Casual, my mother says; Denim and Khaki, no sparkly things to make them shine. Dull, I guess you'd say."

Your mother would know, Audi was thinking but she didn't say it. She and Nash had a long way to go in saving their friendship. The others had no interest in learning about Acorn, anyway. They were watching the Hughes family farm's intention to bring a piece of equipment through the downtown street that would cover both lanes and stop traffic.

"My Daddy," Bentley whispered, "says the Hughes farm has no other entry to their land that lays around Perish than to use the Main street entrance, unless they drive out of the way and come in from the North but other farms won't allow it, one in particular, Mr. Raymond Long."

"Can't no one get along," Audi's opinion was still a bit jaded and Nash was on the opposite bench.

"There's that man, our mommas were talking about," Suz whispered. "Shh. Don't say anything."

Jacob Long came walking toward them. He had driven the truck for Lonnie Hughes on the backroads. It helped Lonnie, but Jacob not having a driver's license could not drive through Troy Sander's town. He and Lonnie were not sure if Troy, Chief of Police of Perish was in Raymond's pocket or not. Although in the old days Jacob and Troy were friends it was better to be safe than sorry.

"Look at this," Jacob stopped a good length of space from the girls. "Five little flowers out early this morning. What would bring such pretty little flowers out on the street this early?" He tipped the baseball cap he wore and placed it back securely on his head. "How ya'll doing?" The girls giggled but not one answered. "Oh, well now," Jacob said, "I see these flowers don't talk. Ya'll have a good day."

"I like him," Audi said

"Be careful, though," Nash, the authority on all subjects warned. "There's word going around about him."

"Did your Momma start it?" Audi asked. Nash glared at her and moved away. Audi laughed. "One for me." Nash was assembling the girls in a line. She didn't speak when she arrived to Audi, just pointed. Audi stepped in place and moved with the girls. "Where we going?"

"To examine the car where the scrap of material was, remember? Bentley said it was in the crack of the car bumper and it looked like Lily's dress."

It wasn't far. They found an elderly lady, a bit bundled up, sitting on the front porch. "Ma'm," Nash said with an air of importance, "We would love to examine your car. We are doing a study on the older makes and models and we heard yours was one of a kind. May we?"

Audi listened in admiration. She would give it to Nash; she had a way with words.

"Don't raise the hood," the woman said, "I can't have it falling on you."

The girls walked slowly around the car, with Bentley laying a finger on the hairline crack. The material had become a few threads. They finished their inspection and Nash decided to speak with the woman.

"Excuse me, Ma'm, do you still drive this car?"

The woman laughed. "I'm not allowed to drive for a while; according to my doctor my blood pressure is over the moon." She thought for a minute before she spoke again. "I believe my vehicle was driven around the time that little girl was misplaced."

"But you said you can't drive right now."

"It wasn't me. I went in to the Funeral Parlor. You know you can pay for your final service through the years and it won't hit the family so hard when the time arrives. Well, that's when I had the spell, sweat, heart poundin' at first then nothing and the girl from the funeral parlor called my doctor. He said I needed to get right in there, to his office. So I'm thinking who I can get to drive me, now.

Raymond Long was coming in the door. "What's goin' on?" He asked and she told him I needed to go to the hospital right then. "I couldn't believe him sayin' he would take me. I thought well, I'm going to ride in that big black hearse with my eyes open this time." She paused to glance at each one of them before finishing. "He says no, we'll go in your car." She sighed heavily. "Long story short, Raymond drove me home afterwards and returned to the Funeral Parlor in my car to find no one there to help him return it. He called and said, "Tomorrow, I'll have your car back. Don't you worry and call me if you need me tonight." She smiled as though it was her best memory. "Wasn't that nice of him?"

"Ma'm, do you attend church? We'd like to see you at our First Missionary Baptist Church."

"Remember, young lady, "I can't drive. Would someone pick me up?"

They cleared a good distance from the woman's house when Audi asked, "Why did you invite that woman to church, knowing she can't walk good?" Audi just could not understand Nash. "Who will pick her up?"

"Girls, remember we don't discuss our finding with anyone. This one we have to wait and see."

They returned uptown, intending to sit on the bench again but Jacob Long was sitting there. A board and checkers on the seat beside him. "Either you girls want to play a game?" He asked.

"I will," Bentley replied, "My daddy taught me a bit about it. He said you and him are friends."

Nash's head shot up. How had she not asked that question? That night she said, "Daddy, are you friends with that Jacob Long man?"

"Well, Nash, I think all of us that used to be are trying to decide if we're still friends. Why?"

"Bentley played him a game of checkers right up on Main Street this morning in front of Acorn."

"Jacob and Jared were always friends. Jared doesn't change. He's a loyal friend." He sighed. "I guess that don't say much for me. Yes, I'm Jacob Long's friend. You just settled that question for me."

"How about Lonnie Hughes, was he Mr. Jacob Long's friend?"

"Without a doubt, yes, he was."

Nash thought about the piece of material stuck in that woman's car. She had the license plate number. If someone didn't pick her up for church where they would learn her name, then Bentley would have to ask her daddy to find out, then again the Chief of Police said, keep me informed. Where there was a will there was a way.

The next day when she encountered Chief of Police, Troy Sanders, she knew it was fate. Taking out the notebook, she approached him. "Sir, you said we should stay in touch regarding our investigation."

"Yes, ma'am," he replied. "Do you have something?"

"I do. Could you run this plate number and let us know who this vehicle belongs to?"

"Should I ask if this involves Lily?" He studied Nash. She appeared neither nervous nor scared of his badge.

"Not at this time," she replied in a serious voice. "Should it prove useful we will inform you. Thank you."

He humored the girls and ran the plate himself and reported to Nash after school. "That plate was in the name of Mrs. Dawsey Koonce," he waited for her reaction. To her credit, Nash showed no emotion.

"Thank you," she said. He watched her walk away to join her friends. Then he made a note in his phone.

Love suffers long and is kind....

Chapter 5

The call came in at seven thirty, Deputy Jacks could handle it. Troy Sanders was ready to leave. Luann called early to say, "We're having fried chicken just like you ask for, honey, mashed potatoes, the works. I expect you to be here."

"White gravy?" Troy was mentally rubbing his stomach. Too many late nights home and cold food made him appreciate Luann's effort tonight. He heard Jacks calling. "I gotta go, Babe, see you in a minute."

"The lady won't tell me the problem, Sir. She's crying and very distraught but insists on speaking with you." He hand the phone over to Troy.

"Troy Sanders, here. How may I help you?"

"Troy, this is Charlotte. Mother's gone." Sobs she was trying to control, Troy guessed, came across the line. "I've looked everywhere, drove down the street, went by the city pond. She's hiding out, Troy. Lately she thinks someone's out to get her…" Charlotte's voice dropped to a whisper, "since Lily died."

"She hides from you?"

"She doesn't even know who I am at those times, Troy. Sometimes I wonder if she knows something about Lily being taken that night and the distance scares her…it's almost a mile from here, isn't it? The bench?"

Troy was listening as he motioned his men around the desk. "Maybe so, Charlotte. We will put the men out on the streets, and knowing Perish, as soon as word is out, the citizens will show up for a walk through the community."

"I'm embarrassed to make this call, Troy, but if I don't Mother may fall into real peril."

Later, after his men were informed and a plan established, Troy remembered that word. Peril. Perish and peril, it seemed went together.

"Be careful and considerate how you handle Mrs. Granger," he said. To the men, "One tragedy in that family is enough. Charlotte's a strong woman but sometimes even a strong chain breaks."

Ten thirty arrived, dark had settled. The news carried Mrs. Granger's disappearance and that brought the community. The late November night also brought need for jackets. Margie Burke and her neighbor came to the station. Troy had returned from the first city search. "It's going to rain," Margie said. "What then?"

"Mrs. Granger is probably scared to death. She's out there without a coat and it's getting cooler. I doubt it rains and the weather channel didn't mention it. "We don't need that Margie. What we do need is someone to man the phones. You did that for twelve years. Could you do it tonight?"

Margie glanced to Edward. They were more than neighbors. Troy broke in quickly, "You'll need backup, Margie. Think you could teach Edward?"

"Same system?" She was staring at the station where she'd sit for twelve years. She remembered it.

"Yeah, it is." With all the men out in the field, no one was manning the phones, except him. Trying to coordinate the search, keep his men informed and the station open was getting to him. He needed to be out on the field with the people of Perish. Jacks was supposed to stay and Pitts was on vacation?

"That system should've been discarded long ago, Troy, right out the door."

"If it had been, Margie, there wouldn't be an expert like you ready to take over right now."

"Go do what you have to do, Troy. Me and Edward will be just fine. But take a raincoat. It's going to let loose in a down pour. Probably, you got an hour, but after that…my bones aren't aching for nothing."

* * *

It was eleven thirty when Charlotte heard the knock on the door. Timid, at first, then a regular tap tap of the knuckles she guessed. She motioned the person inside. Dark clothes, a hood over the head, she didn't recognize who it was but she felt strongly this person was part of the search. Troy had told her to stay home in case her mother returned, but four hours had passed and that wasn't likely.

"Charlotte?"

A smattering of chill raced down her spine. She knew that voice, one she least expected.

"Charlotte, I think I know where your mother is." Jacob stood before her removing the hood. "You need to get a warm coat, maybe a raincoat, the wind has changed and there's moisture in it."

"Why are you helping search?" Charlotte was surprised but mostly apprehensive. "You and mother never agreed. You practically hated each other."

"She hated me. I disliked her ways of dealing with our marriage, Charlotte. You may not like me either but at least be fair."

"My daughter is missing," she screamed. "Both of my daughters. Do you understand? I can't stand this, anymore, being reasonable, saying what's right." She glared at him. "What is right, Jacob. What you did, was that right? Taking Macie, making me sign papers I would never see her again." She turned. "Get out." Her voice carried through the house, through empty rooms that almost echoed.

"Do you still have that old Gator? Does it run?" At least he remembered to just keep to the point, ignore the ranting and soon Charlotte would come through to what really mattered.

She gaped at him. "Are you crazy? Coming in here, asking about some old piece of nonsense? I heard you weren't allowed transportation, but this…this is even beneath you. Yes, it runs."

"Then get your jacket and let's go." Jacob saw the hatred in her eyes, nearly as strong as her resistance he reckoned. She was ready to fly apart, her nerves were shattered. He'd seen her that way before; the day he took Macie. "Do you want to find your mother, before it rains?"

They stared at each other, the one, confused why he was there; hating him for taking from her what she loved most, the ire of him to come when she was in panic, another member of her family missing.

He saw beyond the hatred, her raw emotions and the distrust. How could she trust him? He held out his hand, palm up. "Place your hand there, Charlotte, where it was once when we cared, when we tried, when we trust." Weary, his head dropped, framing words brought fatigue faster than anything else. "I'm not here to hurt you, Charlotte but to help."

* * *

It had taken some doing, getting Charlotte to accompany him. He had to be careful. Even his friends might turn against him if he appeared to be trespassing on land he was forbidden to enter. "Why were you there?" He could hear them pressing for answers. But this, this was something he felt almost certain of, or he wouldn't have come to Charlotte's home, a home in days and years past he had visited on occasion, though it was clear he was not wanted. Where they were going would be a revelation to Charlotte, one she had never known. Something kept rolling through his mind that needed explaining.

"Charlotte, what did you mean when you said both your daughters were missing?"

She gave him a blank stare. "Did I say that?" He nodded. She tried to remember. "Are you sure I didn't say my mother was missing?" His eyes were troubled. For a moment she remembered days when things were different. Once she loved him but he changed and then when their daughter was cut off from her life and the injustice slapped her in the face day after day; she had hated anyone connected to that court case. It was a drummed up mess, using society's intervention to push home his merits and tear down hers. Nothing was fair. She had nearly died of misery. Her arms were empty, his were full. Now he questioned her. How could he have the gall to question her? A cold heart would not understand. But she would reply. That was who she was.

"It feels like Lily is missing. She hasn't merely died to this world. I look for her. I cannot find her."

"What happened to your faith?" He shrugged when she gave him a cold hard stare. "I'm not questioning it. You were strong in that regard. I wasn't."

"You should have been," she replied. "Your parents brought you up to know where to place your trust. Isn't trust in God the definition of faith?" She jerked her shoulders forward, a shield to ward off what was happening. "For God's sake, Jacob. You of all people question my faith."

An almost mocking tone entered her words. "How would you feel, your life destroyed by someone else's actions. In my case yours. Had it not been for believing God would carry me through I would have died, maybe carelessly seeking comfort or simply put… a way out. I ask Him why? Why have you allowed this? She faced Jacob, her mouth a straight line, her eyes hard. "You have no idea. I was destroyed. I should have died. I couldn't sleep. I didn't eat. I mourned. I cried and I hated you, the one I was supposed to trust, the one who promised to stand by my side through sickness and health to death." It came to her, her words were useless. "You will never know, Jacob."

He gave a bitter laugh. "I know. For years I didn't and then suddenly I lost everything. People I thought I could trust took my freedom, my possessions, but most of all my dignity…what scrap I had left. You think I don't know….I walk because someone said I was incapable of driving…I am checked on by people who use my money to keep tabs on me…I am left to find a scrap of joy wherever it has been left unattended because I'm a derelict, unwanted, a lunatic some might say, because I was wounded in the head and things are not as clear as they were once…living death…yes, I understand better than you think." His words, too many, he thought, tightening his hand on the wheel, avoiding a bump, sinking the gator for a moment in a deep rut as they covered the mile, to the forest where he knew Mrs. Granger would be. She was silent. Had she heard him? He had not said he was sorry. She would not believe his words. He was surprised to be allowed near her. She was distraught or it would not have happened.

* * *

The ride was complete. They arrived at a clearing of sorts, their view a line of trees that shield the eye from seeing what lay beyond but when the wind blew, almost Charlotte could imagine the outline of a house or a cabin, which she wasn't certain. The path was no clearer for navigation than had been the road they traveled. An ordinary car would not have made the ride but perhaps a four wheel drive vehicle could. She wondered if the location was miles away from her mother's home or within traveling in a short length of time if one knew the way, for there had been many small roads running into the one.

She finally spoke. "How in the world would my mother have known this place and how would she have walked to it if she is here as you strongly suspect?"

"Come; let's see if we can get across these deep ruts. As you can see others travel these roads which when I realized your mother might come here worried me exceedingly." He drew a deep breath as if to clear his very person of something dreadful and it really in fact was the stress and strain the hour had laid upon him. It was true he did travel the backroads to keep from being shamed before others. He was supposed to have achieved fame, but what famous person was seen on foot? He knew the back roads like the palm of his hand and so had Mrs. Granger. Situations between them at times had grown so bad, he had followed her on occasion to this very spot to see what she was up to and it was here they had reached treaty of sorts to her dislike for her daughter's husband, specifically him.

"You're not good enough for her," she had said that first day he found her, puttering away placing items in different locations of the house. "You will leave her when your private person is exploited and becomes society's child."

"What in the world are you saying?" He had asked.

She replied, "There's a fidgetiness about you, you do lip service to most people only because you long for and anticipate being that society's child I spoke of."

"Never," he said then, but now he wondered how did she know? Years later, the words reverberated in his mind. "Why don't you like me?"

"For what I just said. Charlotte is an only child, perhaps a spoiled one in some regards because she is the only one, or maybe because she is all we have. We want what's best for her. You will never stand with her."

"I suppose you have a crystal ball to predict the future," he had said, sarcastically.

"I have wisdom," She replied, tapping her forehead. "I'm not sure you will ever get it unless you channel your thoughts and act wisely upon the good ones. Your constituents are frauds."

He was enraged that she suggests such ridiculousness. "No, our relationship was not without flaws," he said. He didn't realize he'd brought the past to the present and spoke out loud until Charlotte gave him a strange look that said are you talking to yourself or to me. "Sorry about that, I was thinking of your mother."

"What is this place and who does it belong to?" She was instantly suspicious. "My mother would never be able to walk here." She saw his dubious glance. "And no, she wouldn't be capable of hiring anyone. She is frail, Jacob. Her mind explores night and day and her body tries to keep up. My mother is, brittle. She could never have made it this far. We hear of the energy of dementia patients. They either go listless or like Mother have the energy of ten. But she could not make it this far."

"Really? Then let us go inside." A thought entered his mind. "Has your mother unleashed that energy on you?" She ignored him. He walked up the steps and opened the front door. "She refuses to lock it."

"You've been here?" Her voice was incredulous at the thought. "I have never heard of this place."

"When we were married I stumbled upon it. Your parents didn't want me in their home but I could roam their woods, and lo and behold, I stumbled upon it and there was your mother very much the queen of domain. There was something wrong, even then. She greeted me in as though we were old friends. "Elizabeth," he called out to the empty house. "Elizabeth, we are here."

"You called my mother by her first name?" She rolled her eyes. "This is unbelievable. What a farce."

There was a movement that reminded Jacob of a chair scooting away from a table and then, there she was, "Elizabeth Granger," he announced, bowing as Charlotte's mother entered the room.

"Charlotte, dear, and Jacob. How nice you have come to visit but your father's not home, dear."

Her hair was in such disarray. Her clothes appeared to have the scars of travel through brambling bushes. There was a huge knot over her left eye. Still, she gave a curtsy and smiled, coming first to peck a kiss on Charlottes cheek and then Jacob's. Charlotte saw the dirt under her fingernails. It had not been an easy trip. The scratches on her arms were deep and raw, though she seemed not to notice.

"You like him?" Charlotte exclaimed. "I mean, do you always greet your visitors with a kiss on the cheek?" Charlotte's mind was in a whirl.

"Mother, we've been worried over you. You've been missing a number of hours and we couldn't find you."

"I was right here, Charlotte, in this little house your father built for me in the woods. "Dear," he would say, "you seem a bit on over load. What do you need? What would make you happy?" She smiled. "I want a house in the woods, just a playhouse that when my mind seems ready to explode I can go there." Her laughter reminded them of a happy giddy child. "He loves me. I don't know where he is right now."

"We have to return home, Mother. It's past midnight. The Police are looking for you."

"Police?" Her expression turned to fear. "I haven't done anything wrong. Why do they look for me?"

"It's all right, Mother." Charlotte wondered how to handle the situation. "We really need to start back. It may rain any minute."

Elizabeth Granger huffed, petulant as an angry child. "I won't go. Who cares if it rains?"

Jacob saw her attitude changing. "Hey, Lizzy, girl, let's you and me and Charlotte take a gator ride."

"Can I drive?" She glanced toward the back hall. "Is Daddy going with us, shall we find him?"

"Not this time, there's threat of rain. Remember those ruts?" Jacob reached out claiming her hand. "We need you to put on your coat. Are you ready?" She nodded. "Then let's go."

* * *

"You sit in the back," she instructed Charlotte. "I'll help Jacob drive." Without further thought she rubbed the knot over her eye. "It hurts," she said, as if they had asked. "I fell and there was a big old rock. Does it look like it hurts, Jacob?"

"Yes, Lizzy girl, it does. I bet you kicked that old rock, didn't you?"

She giggled and ran her hand through his arm at the elbow. "I like this part when we ride home."

"Weren't you with Daddy, Mother? I doubt you and Jacob ever rode together."

Mrs. Granger replied, "Maybe it was Daddy. I forget. I'm so tired."

Jacob patted his shoulder. "Lay your head right there, Lizzie girl."

"Have you always been good to me, Jacob?" Mrs. Granger tried to suppress a heavy yawn.

"No, Lizzie. You and I had different views on life."

"Well, you seem like a nice man. I thought maybe you were there that morning with me and Lily when we sit on the bench and waited for the bus…but something happened. I can't remember what it was but Lily was upset and always if one of mine was I was upset too."

Almost asleep due to the drone of the gator's motor and a certain vibration to the seat, suddenly Charlotte took notice of her mother's words. "Why were you upset, Mother?"

"I don't know why we were. It wasn't good. That man said, "Come on Miss Granger I'll take you home. Only he said, "I'll carry you home. I remember thinking that would be nice, but he quit talking to me, but to Lily he said, you wait right here I'm gonna take your grandmother home and bring back your Momma."

"Now, why did he leave her there? To catch the bus?" Mrs. Granger pondered her own question. "I know he went back and gave her more juice after he put me in the gator. It wasn't this gator was it, Jacob? Because his gator had only a front seat."

* * *

"Do you think of that time often, Lizzie girl?" The first drops of rain bounced on the hood of their transportation; the ruts in this area were deep where teenagers went on weekends to test their skills. Jacob waited for Mrs. Granger's reply. "Does this weigh heavily on your mind?"

She yawned again. "I don't recall worrying over it but I think now and then I don't know who he was and I keep thinking I'll ask Lily who was that man. I don't remember well, anymore." She clutched Jacob's arm. "Sometimes I don't believe I remember anything and then there are times like now."

"Mother did you take Lily to the bench to wait for the bus?" Mrs. Granger ignored Charlotte.

"Daddy told me not to tell Charlotte. She would be worried and it might hurt her feelings we didn't invite her along, Jacob. Can you keep a secret? Daddy was with us, he said, "you can drive it, Hon, you always wanted to and this is your time." She sighed "he always said that, "this is your time."

The rain that held back was now pelting their faces. Jacob knew he had to stay out of the ruts and find the right road to Mrs. Granger's home. They were in danger because no one knew they had taken the ride through the woods. The distance was not great but the condition of the road was hazardous. If Mrs. Granger became ill, Charlotte would lose her this time. It wasn't just her mind that was frail, as Charlotte had said, the woman was failing. He wondered that Charlotte had handled the situation this far. The rain quickened to a down pour as Elizabeth Granger began to cry, a doleful sound at first, increasing to a grieving that built and erupted in to a storm of sobbing she could not control.

"Why didn't we bring him? He stays there in that house in the woods and I have to go find him and where is Lily? She said she would never stray but that night she was going to find him for me." The sobbing would not stop. Jacob saw the road and thanked God home was not far away. He was weary beyond measure. If he could hang on…just hang on…

* * *

Never had the lights of home been more welcoming. That she had the forethought to leave them on was in itself a miracle on this night. They had progressed to a new day by God's sheer mercy, Charlotte thought as the Gator came to a stop at the garage door. She slid from the back seat to give the combination to open the door and Jacob pulled inside out of the rain. Charlotte tried to call Troy but there was no service. She held up the phone for Jacob to see, shaking her head. He seemed to understand.

They were all soaked. How could Elizabeth Granger be asleep under such horrific conditions? Jacob eased away from where her head lay on his shoulder, his own body trembling beneath the effort. There had been many times he had to accept his own limitations but tonight had been a grueling task, his head was pounding and his heart felt as though a hundred pound weight set on his chest.

"Charlotte," he surveyed the sleeping form of her mother. "In other days I could have carried her in but my muscle strength has waned, how can we do this?" His voice sounded sad to his own ears. "She is soaking wet and we must get her in the house. Without a doubt the rain sent all the others to their homes and Troy must be wondering where we are."

"Mother. Mother." Charlotte pulled her mother to the edge of the seat. "Mother, wake up. It's time for a warm bath and then to bed." Elizabeth Granger appeared as a confused child, her eyes opened in alarm, staring with unseeing eyes at the two of them. "Mother, ease off now and lean on me."

Opening the door to the house, Jacob stood aside as a struggling Charlotte bent to the task, her own clothes dripping water, sagging beneath the dead weight of her mother as they made the steps one at a time, gripping the short rail she had installed for moments such as this she had not yet experienced.

"Help me, Jacob, through the house to her room. There's a chair by the shower and we will sit her there until I get the water temperature just right." As though they had practiced many times the two went through the motion. He turning away as Charlotte tuned the tap, stripped Elizabeth Granger's clothing and crawled into the shower with her. "The second drawer, Jacob of the dresser, a clean gown. Get a warm one."

He opened the drawer to a neatly folded stack of garments and drew out a flannel gown. "Now, turn back the bed covers," Charlotte instructed. "I'll dry her off and it will take us both to lift her up."

It had taken thirty minutes and seemed an eternity with her mother too confused and groggy to help. Charlotte's strength was gone as now she studied Jacob a folded heap in the chair her mother vacated for the shower, elbows on the arms of the chair he held his head in his hands and the pain she read on his face drove home the man's despair. Whatever the main issue of his health, he had given every inch of himself to bring her mother, to bring them all home. She could not forget the past nor forgive him but she could give credit to his effort on this night. She could never have handled this task by herself.

She had pinned the weeks scripture of the love chapter on the bedside lamp for her mother, *love is long suffering and kind.* Subconsciously, she pushed back years of hardship and misunderstanding.

"Jacob, step into the shower. I will find clothes for you. You know where the guest room is down the hall." He was staring at his feet as if they were foreign objects. She stooped to untie the laces, eased the soaked shoes from his feet and helped him to stand. "There," again she turned the tap, waiting for the warmth of the water. "Drop your clothes, Jacob and step in. I'll bring towels and clothes for tonight."

He was in the shower when she returned with Jack's old sweats, they would do, possibly even fit, both men were tall and lean. She saw his form through the steamed glass doors, his back to her, his hands over head practically one with the tiles as he did his best to stand and let the water pour over him. "Here are towels, Jacob. I'm going to my room to shower. If you need anything, perhaps you will remember where things are kept."

It never occurred to her to feel fear, now that they were in the safety of home while the wind rose and rain continued to pelt the windows, the storm within their personal lives this night held everything else at bay. It required every last ounce of strength to set the water for herself, dry off and step into sweats. But there was one last check on her mother before she fell onto the bed. She shuffled down the hall. Her mother's moans reaching her ears. How many nights did she rise, to whisper in her mother's ear. She was sure she heard the moans even when she was in the shower. The door was still partly ajar as she had left it. There stretched half across, his feet dangling off the bed, a sleeping Jacob held her mother's hand. No doubt he thought to comfort her before going to the guest room but Charlotte's mother had a death grip on his hand and in waiting for it to loosen, Jacob fell asleep. There was nothing she could do, Charlotte stumbled back to her room and fell on the bed. She was asleep before the sheet touched her body.

Love does not envy

Chapter 6

They had heard the sirens during the late evening. "Is there a storm?" Bentley asked her mother. The reply made her want to call Nash but phone service was out. When her mother went to her room for the night, Bentley hurried down the steps to the basement and out the door nearest to Nash's home. She tapped on the window, knowing if Nash was there she would let her in. Sure enough, Nash opened the window and pulled her into the room. "Shh," she whispered. "My mother is here but Daddy is still out on the search."

"What search? My dad hasn't come home," Bentley replied, "Mother said it's some kind of community problem. I asked what kind and she said, nothing for you to worry about and that made me worry. Do you know?"

Nash glanced toward the door, "Before the power went off I heard my mother on the phone. She said there was a community search for Mrs. Granger, Lily's grandmother." The girls stared at each other. "You remember how she would come out and sit and just stare into the distance and once or twice she said, I wish Lily would come home and Daddy, I always feel better when he's here."

"Lily's mother always took her back inside so I didn't hear that but she was different."

"It's like if she's lost in memory," Nash explained. "She lives in the past, my mother says. Something has happened to her mind and maybe she went outside today and forgot to go back in. No one knows and they can't find her."

Bentley shuddered. "Daddy would have told me but Mother thinks everything upsets me these days." She sighed. "Does it scare you, Nash? I mean, Lily was found on that old bench in the middle of the night and now her grandmother is out in the dark?" A loud crash of lightening made the girls jump. "I better run home, if my mother looks for me she will panic and I don't want lightening to strike me."

"If we can, let's meet in the morning, maybe we could go into City Hall, since your daddy's mayor."

"We can't meet unless power is restored. I don't think anyone has phone service." Bentley replied.

But the power was on and phone service working when Nash called the other three the next morning. Now, as though it was nothing unusual, the girls were in the entrance of City Hall. "I came early," Bentley whispered, "and Daddy says no one has heard from Mrs. DeLang."

"Isn't that odd?" Audi asked. "I keep remembering what the Sheriff said, if one little girl goes missing, what about the next? Maybe it wasn't those words but that's what he meant. Except this is an old woman? Is there a connection?"

Suz had held back long enough. "I heard my momma and daddy talking. That man who called us little flowers told Lonnie Hughes he thought he knew where she was and my daddy said how would he know, but Momma saw me and said, Suz, you don't go telling anything we say because we don't know a thing. But now you mention that man."

Galanti usually the one to hold her thoughts to herself, wore a puzzled expression when she asked, "Did you know that man that called us flowers was once Mrs. Delang's husband?"

"His name is Jacob," Nash corrected. "Her dead husband's name was Jack. Remember her telling our mothers? He was a preacher."

"He was a minister," Audi added.

"Same thing," Nash agreed, "Where did you hear your information, Galanti? Did someone say that?"

"My daddy was cleaning out his desk and found old pictures. There was one of Mrs. Delang when she was young and I thought it was him, he was smiling and happy looking and I said Daddy who is that? He said, "Why that's Jacob Long before he got hit in the head."

"Why is Mrs. Delang with him?" I asked. "And my daddy said they were married, then my Momma calls to daddy from across the room and they give each other a funny look and daddy says, "don't repeat that, honey."

"Why would your daddy have that picture?" Nash wasn't certain this conversation held merit.

"They were friends. All our daddy's were friends to Jacob Long."

"Well, some don't act like it," Audi was shaking her head. "If they were friends, they'd treat him better. He has to walk ever where he goes, some pick him up but others won't. Is that a way to treat a friend?"

"Well sometimes you're pretty hateful to me." Nash retorted.

"We're not talking about you," Audi snapped. "I don't care whether you believe it or not. I do."

"If he looked so happy, why didn't they stay together?" Nash asked. "I think that needs explaining."

"Does it have anything to do with our investigation?" Audi's eyes were drawn to a point, "Or not?"

Nash ignored her. "Did any of you hear they did an autopsy to determine Lily's death?"

"You seem to have all the news, Nash. Why don't you just tell us? That sounds important so why would Mrs. Delang keep it to herself?"

"The pain," Bentley said softly. "It's not what a mother wants for her little girl. My Momma told me and I promised not to tell." Her eyes held a sadness she had seen in her mother's eyes. "I don't think she wanted to but the Sheriff said Mrs. Delang, there's not a broken bone in her body. I don't think someone ran over her. I think there's more to it. No doubt someone found her, who is the question"

"How long have you sit on this information?" Nash demanded, her authority was slipping. "I declare, Bentley, did you know this last night?"

"Last night, Nash, when Daddy came home. The question is, when did you find out and were you going to tell us?"

Audi was horrified. "Did they dig up Lily's body?" Tears were forming in her eyes.

"No, they did it before she was buried. Lot of people knew but they swore not to tell."

"If no one ran over Lily," Suz whispered, "Does that mean maybe there's not a mean person in our town doing terrible things?" She swallowed nervously, "Can we sleep good again, knowing no one hurt Lily?"

"There's still someone knows what happened, Suz." Bentley reached across for Suz hand. "Somebody knows but they're afraid to speak up. Someone still had to place Lily on that bench and why in the night?"

Suz stared across to Audi, knowing they'd both had nightmares and other problems. "I don't like this. I think it's getting scarier than better. I wish we'd never decided to investigate. I move we quit."

"We haven't done any good, anyway," Bentley added. "It just makes us think of Lily more."

"Was Lily our friend?" Nash pushed home the real reason they decided to investigate. "Was this our way of saying so? I think we need to watch these people more closely. Let's make a list of names."

* * *

Charlotte awakened to the sound of the washing machine. Surely her mother was not recovered enough to be doing laundry. Trying to unwind herself from the bed covers, she realized she had died to the world once her body touched the sheets. She could only wonder how her mother would feel having made it through the night, followed by the fact Jacob was in her home. How did that happen?

She stumbled down the hall, peeped in to see her mother was still asleep and padded on down the hall to the kitchen. A pot of coffee was brewing and by the cook top there was an assortment of eggs, a box of pre-cooked bacon and a toaster with two slices of bread ready to go under.

"Good morning, Charlotte. I trust you slept well." There was a hint of a smile about his lips and his eyes twinkled. She wondered, was this what he meant that he found joy when least expected or deserved?

"Morning," she replied, taking her usual mug from the cabinet, the one with her name sprawled white letters over a red background. Charlotte. Sometimes she thought that mug told her story, if it was full meant she had time to linger but half empty meant one of two things, get over this mess and move on, or looking into her own stained cup she spent too much time chastising decisions she had made or ignored.

"How do you want your eggs?"

"Scrambled."

"One or two slices toast?"

"One." She watched him press the lever to the toaster and then break eggs into a buttered skillet. "You remembered where everything's kept?"

He shot her a questioning glance. "Yeah, I have a head injury that creates havoc on occasion but I don't have complete memory loss though sometimes I wish I did." She was silent. "There are times," he explained, "I can't believe my life has taken this turn. I thought I'd play ball a few years, retire to a good business…maybe do a bit of traveling." He sighed, "Well returning to your home town a failure is not the same."

"Who says you're a failure?" She laid paper napkins by each place, silverware, a jar of jelly from the frig. "Perish doesn't have a lot of unsung heroes. There was a time the community held great pride in you."

"I suppose coming from you I should take that as a compliment but we both know it isn't." The toaster buzzed as he was turning the scrambled eggs onto plates. The precooked bacon beeped in the microwave and she brought it to the table. "Toast," he said, "and breakfast is served." They sat down together.

"This is new," he stared across the table, "never thought we'd sit together again." He reached for her hand as he bowed his head. "Father, we thank you for a new day, for your blessing of safety and comfort and this food. Bless the food to our bodies and our bodies to your love and mercy. Amen."

"Now you pray?" She eyed him curiously to see if it was another one of his ploys, but he seemed sincere.

"Yeah, one of the things I learned after I wore myself out trying to fix things I couldn't fix."

She wasn't lost to Jacob's explanation. Hadn't she done the same? The troubling period between his leaving, taking Macie, meeting Jack and a quick marriage were part of a time of great unrest and trying to find her way. If it hadn't been for Jack, she let the thought claim her, if it hadn't been for Jack she would have perished. So black was that season of her life she had tried to shut it away but a person always had to deal with pain or it would kill you. Jack saved her from herself when she thought she had no reason to live.

"You attend church, Charlotte?"

She nodded. "I did, before Lily…"

"What about now will you again?" He raised his head to study her, his own expression serious, his eyes as troubled as her own. "I tried the church where my parents went before they had to move, but it didn't feel right, then Lonnie talked me into this one," he gave a weary shrug. "Somethings' missing, its probably in me, but I sit there on the back pew, all the others seem of one accord but I don't know where I fit in or if I ever will again."

"I was going there."

"I know, Lonnie told me after I went the first two Sunday's." He reached for the coffee pot. "More?" She nodded. "Do you ever feel the rest of the world has passed you by and you're running to catch up?"

"Catch up, measure up, be as good as the next person all the while feeling like I'm the only one with this blight on my head. Blaming myself," She placed her napkin on the table, "Blaming you."

In spite of the uncomfortable moment between them, their bodies craved food. The silence in the kitchen was broken only by the ticking clock on the wall. She reached across to check the phone. "Still dead," she muttered. "We have to let Troy know." She let the sentence drop, finishing finally to say, "life has so much misery, worry and unanswered questions, things we didn't see coming. It's like trash it keeps popping up and you carry a part of it with you because you don't know where to put it."

"A person can't carry garbage the rest of their life, Charlotte. Forgiveness brings relief and carrying it is the worst sickness a person can bear. I know because I experienced it with those who robbed me."

"You can talk about forgiveness as if it comes easily. It doesn't. There's a lot of bitterness." She glanced away, seeing through the window puddles of water on the road leading to the house. "When someone has robbed you of what you love most, you don't know how to turn loose, you carry that baggage." Her words grew thick, "You imply material gain, I was victim of society's lies taking my child and giving her to the greatest imposter of all."

She laid the napkin in her plate, rising to leave him sitting there. "This was not good for me. Somehow I can't compare the loss of a loved one to prestige and power." Bitterness accented her words. "Perhaps we both realize material things do not make one happy but wrongs not made right are like a festering sore. I can't put it down. There's no comparison in losing wealth to losing a child. Thank you for breakfast. I need to check on Mother."

"I've changed, Charlotte. I'm not the same man."

"We'll see," she said. "At this point there's not much I can do. It's all in your field, Jacob."

She turned at the door, her eyes cold. "I need a map of the area we covered last night. Can you handle that?" He nodded. She pointed to pen and paper on the counter. "Don't forget."

* * *

Troy Sanders stared at the phone in his hand. The Sheriff's department was on the way over. "Tell me why you are coming to Perish," he'd said to Wade Bradford but the reply was not satisfactory. "I could spit ten penny nails," he said. Deputy Pitts was listening. "Bad news," Troy said, "what'da you bet it has to do with little Lily? But get this, they aren't coming here, they want to meet at City Hall."

"Love does not parade its self, is not puffed up"

Chapter 7

From the sixth grade class room windows, Nash saw the Sheriff's vehicle drive by. She glanced at the clock behind Miss Poole's desk. The bell would ring in five minutes. She started getting her things together. Bentley turned to stare at her. "Did you see that?" She mouthed. "The Sheriff?" Nash nodded and gave a slight jerk of her head toward Galanti. They would have to track down Suz and Audi from the fifth grade building. Sometimes she wondered if it was worth letting the two younger girls join their club. But then, three was hardly a club and more often than not a trouble spot as the old saying went, two was company and three a crowd. For all her quietness, Galanti could be stubborn.

"Where are we going? Audi asked. "I have to check in with my Momma or I'm in trouble."

Nash hand her cell phone to Audi. "Ask if you can come home with me. MY Mother has a doctor's appointment right about now and time she drives home the Sheriff will have left. We are going to listen in." She glanced at Suz. "Are you good with your Mom?"

"Yeah, she works out of town." Suz was huffing to stay up. "All our moms are trying to make extra money for Christmas, aren't they?" It won't be long; forty three days. I have a count-down calendar."

"What is that?"

"You know, it has little wood squares you take out and move toward the twenty fifth of December, but you can't start using it until first of December so I use the one in the kitchen for now."

"I'd have to see it," Nash replied. "Now, Bentley, they're at the City Hall. It's your dad, there, so you have to get us a place where they won't notice us."

"Why aren't' they going to the Police station? That's where Troy Sanders is. This is not right."

"They don't get along," Nash reasoned, "so what would you do if you were Sheriff?"

"I'd do what was right since I was elected by the people." The girls laughed. "What's funny?" For a minute, Audi felt ridiculed and angry. "What do you all know about it?" She snapped.

* * *

Jared Stiles felt the heat to his face. This wasn't right. It just wasn't right. His friend at the Sheriff's office said, "Now Jared, we've been friends a long time. But this could mean my job if the Sheriff finds out I've tipped you off. I know Jacob is your friend."

"They're just looking for a scapegoat," Jared replied. "There's nothing right about this and you know it."

"I just work here but I thought maybe you needed a heads up before they arrive. They're not going to the Police headquarters, Wade and Troy don't get along, it's always who's higher on the pecking post."

"So they're coming here. Well he's not here."

"They'll bring him in for sure. Gotta go, Jared. Sorry about this turn of affairs."

Jared was running his hands through his hair, trying to figure out his part in the fiasco when he heard Bentley, "Daddy, we have a project we're working on. Can we use one of the rooms?"

"You can," he replied, studying his daughter and wondering how in the world Charlotte Delang was making it after losing Lily. "But we're preparing for an important meeting, you have to stay out of sight and keep it quiet. No giggling or carrying on. You agree?"

"I promise." Bentley motioned the others in from outside.

Jared watched them march by, smiling at each one. "How're you girls this afternoon?"

"Just fine, Mr. Stiles." They were a chorus and he did wonder if letting them stay was the thing to do or not. He closed the door behind them, saying as he did, "Now Bentley you promised." She nodded.

* * *

At the Granger home, Jacob finished cleaning the kitchen, the dishes were in the dishwasher, he wiped down the stove and everything was in good shape. Charlotte had left due to their discussion. He wasn't surprised, nor did he blame her. They were a long way from being friends.

Elizabeth Granger graced the door, surprised but smiling, he said, "Well, look at you. Walking pretty good after that bumpy ride last night." He met her meaning to help her to sit down but she opened her arms and hugged him as though they were bosom buddies.

"I'm so glad you're home, Jacob. No one else takes care of me."

He gave an embarassed laugh. "Charlotte watches over you, Lizzy."

"No, she's mad at me because of Lily." She sighed. "Maybe since you're back with us things will be better."

"You're just confused, Elizabeth." He tried for a more formal approach. "I'll be moving on in a while."

"It's who's to blame for our Lily dying," she said. She saw his puzzling stare. "I'm lucid, right now, Jacob. I know when I am. It's when things start slipping I have no control over my thoughts."

"Elizabeth, Charlotte is sad but she doesn't blame you for Lily's death, and she's not mad. She is grieving."

"Then she should be very angry with me," Elizabeth replied. "We should never have gone out that night."

"Why did you, Elizabeth?"

"I don't know. It is all such a fog. I remember we were searching for someone. Lily was sleepy."

"Think on it, Elizabeth. Maybe it will come to you. For now, I have to dress and go into town to let Troy know you have been found."

"Aren't you staying with us, Jacob?"

"I don't think Charlotte could handle that." Jacob chuckled. "We had breakfast together and that didn't go well. In fact, I left a plate for you, Elizabeth. But I've got to get going."

"Come back, tonight, Jacob and stay with us." She saw his expression. "It's my house, Jacob. Mine."

"You never wanted me around." He was trying to understand the change in his former mother in law.

"I don't remember. I think we need you now. Things are in such an uproar."

Shaking his head, Jacob pulled his clothes from the dryer. "In fifteen minutes you will think differently."

* * *

The ringing of the phone brought Charlotte from the bedroom. "Hmm, so now we have service," she said, answering the phone. "Hello, Troy, yes, we did find mother. Yes, Jacob is here. How did you know?" There was a silence, Charlotte's expression changed as she gripped the phone. Her eyes turned hard and her stare settled on Jacob. "Yes, I'll be glad to drive him in." Hanging up the phone, she said, "They want to see you. The Sheriff and Troy. It's about the night Lily disappeared. Seems there's a witness saw you at the scene that night. There, by the bench, Jacob."

"We will whisk you away, Jacob," Elizabeth said. She was wringing her hands.

"Mother, this is no cloak and dagger game. This is real life and it has to do with the death of my baby, your grandchild."

"He didn't do it," Elizabeth cried.

"Am I suspect?" His voice was quiet, a sadness in his eyes. "If I am, I swear on all that's holy, I am not guilty."

"That will be proven, won't it, Jacob? One way or the other." She shuddered as her mother moaned.

* * *

"Jacob." Troy held out a hand. "We've been waiting for you."

Sheriff Wade Bradford eyed him as though he were looking through a high powered telescope. At the end of a rifle, Jacob was thinking; Sheriff Wade Bradford looked mighty official stretched out in that creased uniform, but Troy seemed a bit wrinkled around the edges. It appeared one's demeanor won the battle. Therefore, if appearance were the main qualifications then Bradford took the prize without a tussle.

"Where you been, Boy?"

Jacob gave Bradford a sizzling glance, ignoring him further when he addressed Troy Sanders, Perish own Chief of Police. "Troy, I believe I heard you were looking for me, and I'm turning myself in to you, not because I'm guilty of anything to do with any of your cases but to cut down on the drama and simply say here I am, now what's the protocol?"

"Now, look here, Troy, you and this boy may already have a plan but it won't work. We came to get this boy and question him." Sheriff Wade Bradford pulled himself to full authority's height, looking down on Troy Sanders, Perish Chief of Police.

"I reckon you will have to wait your turn, Wade. We are going to take care of this matter right here in Perish. There's no warrant out for his arrest, no proof he's broken the law, therefore if it doesn't mess too much with your schedule, we will thank you for your interest and we will take it from here."

"The Prosecuting Attorney will be looking into this matter," the Sheriff replied. "And right away." But for now either you read him his rights or I will." Bradford eyed the two as though they might make a run for it.

"Now Sheriff," Troy said, "He has forty eight hours to show up for that Court hearing and you know it."

"Troy, just because you and Long are friends don't mean you can trust him."

"And can you trust your eye witness, assuming that's why you are wanting to take him in?" Troy asked. "You don't have tangible evidence and yet you come in here like you own the town and intend to take a man's freedom without so much as telling me what you've got. Now is that the right thing to do?"

"Troy, I'm Sheriff of this County. I intend to abide by the law, but no two bit chief of police has authority over me and I'm trying to refrain from cuffing him right here and now in spite of you."

Troy spit on the ground, near enough the Sheriff's boots the dust spattered. "You don't have to get ugly, Wade. We were city police long before you stepped up, that don't mean you don't come from the same stock and caliber as the rest of us, keep up this kind of talk, it'll spread and next election you'll be out out and one of us in just to show you we can do it."

Jacob had listened to the diatribe between the two. "You sound like school boys, who can piss the furtherest," he said. "This being election year, I'm assuming Sheriff you need to bring someone in and me being the lowest on the totem pole and no telling who you are catering too, though I'd guess it's my cousin what wants custody of me so he can spend my money that's being held by higher powers." He watched the sheriff's face turn two shades of red. "I can only imagine what he's promised you. But don't count on it, Sheriff. So it comes down to this. You need someone to blame this crime on. Maybe I'd feel the same but the truth is, I came along a lot later and found that sweet little girl laying on the bench where someone placed her. She appeared in peaceful sleep and I looked around for the adult with her but found no one. Have you questioned the eye witness why they were there, and why they would leave a little girl alone like that?" Jacob shook his head. "But now you say an eye witness saw me there. Am I right, Sheriff?"

Very reluctant the Sheriff nodded. "Yes, and that will be in statement when you come in for your Court hearing tomorrow."

"Statement?" Jacob puzzled. "I'm to appear in person and your witness merely makes a statement?"

"Listen, here, Boy," Sheriff Bradford's irritation spewed forth in his words. "I've about had enough of you."

"I'm not your boy." Jacob's eyes tightened and his expression was grim. "It appears you have already decided I'm guilt without trial." Do you realize your great responsibility to this county could be snuffed out just like that?" Jacob snapped his fingers under the Sheriff's nose. "Have you any idea how it would feel to be reduced to nothing after holding this capacity as a servant to the people of Sand County?"

A bitter smile replaced the grimness of his expression. "Fate happens, Sheriff. People you thought were your friends, turn against you. Someone else comes along thinking they can take care of your business better than you. They can wipe your good record to naught. Next thing you know, you are out and they are in. So don't ride so high and mighty in that uniform you are wearing. You're not here to be judge and jury. You are here to serve the people and that even includes me until proven guilty. Now," he glanced at Troy. "I've got people to notify what's happening with me."

"Who cares about you, Boy?" Sheriff Bradford's words sounded sullen to his own ears.

"You call him that one more time, Wade," Troy interrupted "And I'll have to report you."

"To who?"

"I don't know. Maybe the Prosecuting Attorney's not in your pocket. Who knows? I'd have to study on that. But I'd think if he's in my custody you'd have some more important case to be investigating, like a few dozen you haven't solved yet. Perish is a clean town. We don't need any more trouble or sadness here. I suggest you move along."

* * *

The Sheriff sauntered off to his car, his deputy following. No need hurrying, those standing by wouldn't see him tucking his tail and run. No, Sir, Jacob Long would find what he deserved, tomorrow.

"Troy, I have to ask you something. Do you know anyone willing to drive me about seventy miles tonight? I have to see my parents and check on my daughter. It's one thing to be here in Perish where they can find me, but I saw the blood in the Sheriff's eye and he means to send me down the river."

"He can't do that, Jacob. He'd have me to deal with."

"Think about it, he's probably got the Prosecuting Attorney in his pocket and we don't stand a chance not my innocence or your authority." Jacob stubbed his toe against a rock in the dirt. "There's bound to be loop holes if a man can find them and the Sheriff left here intent to destroy me."

Troy rubbed the full day's growth of whiskers on his chin. "I'd have to go in my private vehicle on my time, but I'll do it." He turned toward the City Hall. "Let me clear this with my deputy. I won't tell him where I'm going that way he won't be part of it. You need anything before we take off?"

"No, I'm good."

* * *

The five stayed as quiet as church mice, leaning in as close to the raised window as they could, to hear. When the car was well out of sight, Audi hopped down from the chair she'd been standing on. "Where are they going?"

Nash replied, "to see his parents and he said daughter. I didn't know they lived seventy miles away."

"There's something about that we should know." Bentley came up off her knees. "I got so tired standing in that strain of my back bent I thought I was going to fall down. Do you remember what Mrs. Delang said about being married to Jacob Long and he took their child from her? I thought that child died. Do you suppose that's who he's going to see, seventy miles away from Perish and Mrs. Delang doesn't even know?"

"I think we need to make a phone call," Nash said. "Not to Mrs. Delang but maybe to her mother. There's information here, that's not ours to sit on but first we have to take an oath we won't tell on each other if we make this phone call. Raise your hands. Do you solemnly swear not to confide, whisper, tell anyone, not one soul we learned this information and passed it one to Mrs. Granger? Do you solemnly swear you are part of this phone call as if you held the phone in your hand and made the call?" Nash eyed each one solemnly. "This could be a matter of life and death to Jacob Long and then what would happen to his dear daughter if his Momma and Daddy died? Keep your hands up. Now, do you swear? All answer by saying I do and crossing your right hand over your heart, so help us God."

"I do." Five I do's resounded in the silence of the big room as Mr. Stiles opened the door.

"Bentley, it's time to go home." He saw the girls with their hands to their heart. "Well, I'm right proud of you girls, pledging the flag. Few people even realize it's there above the door. I'm proud of you."

"Will you make the call?" Bentley whispered as she passed by to join her daddy. Nash nodded. "I will." She said.

* * *

"What's so important you have to see your parents before the hearing? I mean I heard what you said but they've known you were here. Is there a reason you aren't there with them if they need you?"

"You'll see when we get there." Jacob turned to study Troy. "I appreciate this. There's few I can count on. Lonnie, yeah, but he has to stay close with

Beth expecting the baby any day. But Troy, the reason I'm here is I got word Raymond is pushing hard to have custody of me and you know he's a man of standing in his community and even here where they have a second Funeral Home, but I can't have him taking charge of me or what's mine."

"Won't the old man stop that foolishness?"

"You know there's been blight on Oscar's head since he lifted those diamonds off that dead corpse in the casket. Kind of puts a shadow on all morticians, don't it? Truth is, the family shouldn't left them on her and something the community don't know is this, Oscar didn't take those diamonds for his wife to wear, she was bad sick and they'd used up all their savings and the temptation was too strong. There they were something he could sell."

Troy rubbed his chin. "I feel kinda bad now, Jacob. I faced the old man up about that. He was coming down pretty hard about something and I reminded him, I didn't know about his wife." He gave a weary sigh. "I guess a man don't know what he'd do if dire circumstance hit and it was a save your family situation. We love our families. I pray nothing like that ever comes my way."

"Nothing like that going on with Raymond, are there?"

Jacob snorted. "Nothing but pure greed and laziness. He don't even help Oscar but he's there every week to collect his check. You saw that stringy roadside tramp Oscar picked up to train. Well, I can say tramp because I encountered him on my trip over here. Both of us walking. That man has no scruples. I saw him steal from every roadside vendor; you know they are out selling produce right now."

"You traveled together?" Troy studied Jacob and saw he was telling the truth. He was as confounded over the other man's actions as Troy was as a Chief of Police. He saw the type in other towns, but not Perish. Troy was keeping Perish clean. "So you weren't really together?"

"No, we caught different rides and slept that one night in the same town by coincidence, but he left without paying his bill and I didn't have money to pay for him. He had it. He didn't eat the cereal and hot coffee the hotel offered. I saw him in the café on the corner, having a full breakfast."

They rode in comfortable silence conversing now and then.

"What about Charlotte, you got any feeling for her?"

"I can't afford to have. She hates me."

"I don't think Charlotte has it in her to hate anyone. She's just messed up over losing Lily and you would be too." Troy left the thought of the baby Jacob took from Charlotte out of the conversation. "You and Charlotte had a strong love. I'd never have thought it would end."

"I guess it didn't really. I'll always love Charlotte but there's no hope for us with all the problems between us and neither one of us will give. She can hold her anger to doomsday; I'm not giving up Macie."

There, Troy thought, it was said. It was out in the open. "Two parents make a child happy."

"She left me, Troy."

"You divorced her, Jacob. What did you expect her to do?"

"Yeah, well, like I paid for it. Divorced. Hit in the head with a plate to hold my brain in place, and other things….things that sadden a man and make him look back on all his transgressions. That's when I found the Lord, Troy." He glanced at Troy. "Do you know the Lord, Troy? If you don't, I can tell you he's real. When no one else measures up or cares a whit about you He's there and you feel his love and mercy. It's a good thing you nodded, Troy, or we'd have to stop here by the side of the road and bring salvation down on your head." He grew silent and didn't speak again until he said. "Turn here, Troy, three miles up this road is where mom and pops lives."

Troy wondered what had turned Jacob's thoughts away from the day's predicament. Things, he said and it was as if a robe of desperation clothed him, do you know the Lord, he'd said. Yes, Troy thought, I couldn't handle this job if I didn't. Silently he said a prayer for his family at home. But what was the sadness he'd seen in Jacob's face and heard in his voice. *things*. He thought he knew them all, but he guessed he didn't. They'd all know each other since they were kids, but Charlotte had her secrets too. Another thing, in the back of his mind he knew he'd seen Oscar's wife wearing those diamonds. Oscar didn't sell them to take care of his wife. He had just given Jacob another bill of sale. A false one.

* * *

They drove up a lane with white wood fence on each side, a smooth graveled road with a line of trees behind the fence that led up to a deep grassed lawn with a two story A-framed house setting back in the center. The shutters and flower boxes were a medium blue with an abundance of blooming flowers cascading down and the door with a magnificent curved top was stained a deep mahogany to match the steps down from the porch."

Jacob was watching his reaction. "What do you think of our door? Pops made it and it took Mom a month to decide whether she wanted it painted blue or stained. I think the color turned out great."

"It's perfect. Your Dad works well with wood." Troy followed Jacob up the cobblestone path to the house.

"Now he does. There was a time all he did was toil the soil but Oscar ruined that and that time was pure greed in Oscar, but you see how that went, he had to sell the family farm for medical bills later and now a foreigner has control of the land. A nice enough man but he came in here with a pocket full of money just in time for Oscar's need." Jacob was knocking on the door. "Mom's always embarrassed if she has already put on her night clothes, so I'll give her warning."

He opened the door and held it for Troy to enter. "Hey, Pop," he called out. "He'll be in his recliner. Pop, we got company." A frail old gentleman rose up from within the recliner twice his size, and unfolded his body to rise. "That chair used to fit Pop," Jacob said in a low voice. "Man, he's lost more weight."

"Hey, what you doin' here, Son." Fraley Long met his son with a hug. "Who's this? Is that old Troy? Come here, you rascal, I haven't seen you in years." He let go his son and gave Troy a welcoming hug.

"Where's Mom and Macie?" Jacob's eyes were on the door that led down the hall to the bedrooms.

"Why, Son, she was sittin, right there in her chair and heard the tires on the gravel, up she shoots, "Not going to do visiting in this gown she says and off she goes. Now Macie, she's always in her bedroom by this hour watchin Disney, you know." He pointed to the sofa. "Have a seat and tell me what brings you out?"

"It's not good, Pop. They are trying to hang another person's crime on me because they can."

"That ain't right." His father scooted to the edge of the chair. Pain on his face, he asked, "has our distant kin got anything to do with this?" He gave Troy an apologetic glance. "Sorry about that."

"Looks like they're planning for me to be gone awhile, Pops. Can you hold down the fort?" Jacob paused, "I'll leave it to you to tell Mom and Macie but I will tell them I have to leave for awhile."

"Ain't neither one goin' to like it," Fraley shook his head. "What with Macie going in for test." Hearing footsteps coming down the hall he said no more. "Mother, Macie, come see, who's our company."

Macie ran into her daddy's arms. "I thought you were going to be gone awhile."

"I am, but I had to come back to see you. I miss you, muffin." By now a smiling Macie was staring at Troy.

"I miss you, too, Daddy. Is this your friend?"

Troy felt his heart jump and had to control the gasp that ended up stifled in his throat. Macie might have been a year or two older, it was hard to tell because the girl was thin and her skin was a tinge different, almost yellow Troy noted, but she was a replica of Lily, Charlotte's little Lily. How could Jacob not have seen that? How was it he didn't know? Instantly, Troy realized Charlotte for all her silence had kept the secret but Jack Delang was not Lily's father, Jacob was.

"How you feelin, Muffin?" His mother had set on the opposite end of the sofa, leaving the recliner for Jacob. He pulled Macie onto his lap. "You ready for those tests? I sure wanted to be there but they sit them earlier and I can't but you'll call me won't you?" His voice turned serious. "Now, don't worry if I'm hard to reach. I'll get your message but you know I'm not allowed a phone I have to use other peoples."

"I was just waiting to recognize you, Troy? How are you?" Jacob's mother was smiling and happy to see him. "My, Troy, how the years have passed since I baked cookies for you boys."

"I haven't forgotten, Missus Long."

"And now you got that big old title and those fancy uniforms. I declare, Troy, you've done good."

The time passed and Jacob rose. "You better get your rest, Macie." He hugged her tight to his body. "I love you, Muffin. Don't you ever forget that."

"My I wish ya'll didn't have to leave so soon, but I reckon Troy's got his own family to see tonight." Fraley Long was shaking Troy's hand and turning to hug his son. There were tears in both parents eyes.

"I love you, Son," Mary Long said, patting his back as if to comfort them both. "Just trust in the Lord."

"And lean not to thine own understanding," Fraley added in a distraught whisper. "I love you, too, Son."

* * *

"Jacob, why did Charlotte marry that Delang fellow so quick after ya'lls divorce?"

"I'm ashamed of that, Troy. I left Charlotte with an empty bank account, moved everything. Took Macie and left her, distraught and alone; it was much later I realized how overwhelmed she was and didn't know what to do." He sighed. "We'd met Jack through church. In those days we needed church worship but I got nothing out of it, usually hung over or overly tired from a late night on the town that she wasn't with me."

"Jack was an honorable man. Because he was divorced the church wouldn't let him pastor a church but he had such Charisma people flocked to hear him preach, though the church heads called it speaking. He was called to Washington to one of the secondary churches that held a group who frequented White house events. It seemed there were problems within many of the elected officials homes, probably about as consistent as my own, adultery, divorce, mistresses and distraught wives. Maybe that's when I realized what Charlotte went through but by now she had married Jack and gone to Washington with him."

"So you never held animosity toward Jack Delang?"

"I was glad. I'd taken Macie from her and deep down I knew she didn't deserve that. It eased my conscience." He peered across to Troy. "Why the questions? I know you are searching for something."

"As you said, things trouble me. How sick is Macie?"

"Real sick; she needs a kidney transplant but we have no donor."

Love does not behave rudely, does not seek its
own, does not provoke, thinks no evil.

Chapter 8

They rode into Perish. It was ten o'clock. The streets were empty except for one lone car parked in front of the Police Station. "Isn't that Charlottes vehicle?"

"She's the only person I know in Perish that has a Lincoln Navigator."

"What do you make of her being on the street this hour?" Troy turned the key, shutting down the motor and climbed out. "You need anything, Jacob?"

"No, I'll be heading out to Lonnie's. Thanks, Troy. I hope one day I can repay your kindness."

"I guess I better head on over and see what's going on with Charlotte." Troy and Jacob shook hands and Troy headed toward where Charlotte was parked and Jacob rounded the Police headquarters and headed south to Lonnie's.

He hadn't gone far when he heard Troy hollering. "Wait up, Jacob. Wait up." He turned to look back the block he'd already covered.

"You hollering at me, Troy?"

"Yeah, Missus Granger wants to talk to you."

"Elizabeth Granger?" Jacob started walking back. "I don't know what for." She was climbing down out of the Navigator when Jacob reached the vehicle. "What's going on, Elizabeth?"

"I need to talk to you. I got a call I don't understand. I pleaded with Charlotte to bring me over. Some man came out of the Police Department and said you had taken a ride over to Greenway and I waited. I'd have waited until midnight."

"I don't know what this is about, Elizabeth."

"It's about Lily," she paused, "and other things. Let's go over there and sit on that bench in the park. Charlotte's not in the best of mood and she don't know a thing about the call I received."

"Once they were seated, Jacob blew out a breath of hot air and said "tell me Elizabeth. I've been chosen by Sheriff Wade Bradford to come in tomorrow and be arraigned on grounds of responsibility for Lily's death."

"Why that's absurd," she snorted. "You did no such thing. You weren't even there. They might as well take me in."

"Don't say that, Elizabeth. Now, the other thing, what kind of call did you receive?"

"The strangest thing and that voice, I believe I've heard it before, but I can't rightly identify where." She stared into space, "the message was about you. That you were going somewhere; about seventy miles the person said to see your little daughter. Did you know your granddaughter Mr. Jacob Long took from your daughter is no farther than seventy miles from you? That question nearly sent me into hysterics. Jacob, did you and Charlotte have a baby and I've forgotten that important fact or did I never know?"

Jacob rose up from the bench. "This conversation is over Mrs. Granger."

"You might as well sit down, Jacob, I intend to have this information, tonight or I will move Heaven and hell tomorrow to find what I want to know. Now you and I have developed a relationship of sorts this last couple days and it could be we would benefit each other in the long run."

"I doubt that," he replied in a weary voice. "Elizabeth, half the time, you're out of it, either searching for your dead husband or moaning over the loss of only God knows what."

"How harsh. What do you mean I look for my husband?"

"Elizabeth, do you remember the house in the woods, the rain and the deep ruts and coming home soaking wet?"

"What year was that, Jacob?"

He closed his eyes. "Elizabeth, I have a very hard day ahead of me tomorrow."

"Why?"

He shook his head. She had already forgotten he told her tomorrow Wade Bradford would be reading him his rights and if possible sending him either to county jail or farther down the river. He had nothing to lose. He might as well tell her a few of the points and see what happened from there.

"You were not at our wedding. You were not there when we divorced. We lived wherever the team was working. Charlotte and I had a lot of problems and yes, we did have a baby. Her name is Macie. She is very ill and needs a kidney transplant but we have no match for the operation to be performed. She is on a waiting list. Right now there's a possible match but test have to be performed. Elizabeth, today's problems have about bent me double today. Surely you can understand that. I have had enough."

Elizabeth laid a hand on his arm. "I might be a match. Would you let me?"

"You're too old for this kind of surgery and I wouldn't even think of it." He was surprised how lucid and alert she was. He had seen her at her worst and now seemed her best. What brought on the change? In his deepest hopes he had never considered or touched on the merest possibility of this offer. For a moment he prayed the dementia would claim her before she told the story to Charlotte and that would be more turmoil and confrontation than he could face on the night before the arraignment.

"I'm so angry with you and Charlotte. How could you do this to me?" Her tone was accusing and her eyes said the blame lay completely on his shoulders. "How could you take Charlotte's baby away from her? No wonder she went into depression and wanted to die. You left her with empty arms. What kind of man are you, Jacob Long?" She began to cry. His thoughts went back to the moaning of another time.

* * *

He heard the door slam to the Navigator. "Here comes Charlotte." He slumped down onto the bench.

"What have you done to Mother?" She was eyeing him as though he were the world's worst sinner.

"Why did you bring her here?" His contempt was as great as hers. "You knew it would be nothing but trouble at this late hour. What a stupid thing to do." He was tired and tact was out the door.

"What did you say to her?" She insisted, hands on hips, standing before him, her eyes pinpoints and her mouth a straight line. "Why did I bring her? Because I spent three hours listening to her whine, beg, plead, cry and make me a nervous wreck. Have you any idea how many nights sleep I've lost due to her condition? I have no idea what kicked her off tonight but if seeing you would shut her up, so be it."

"Right now, Charlotte, I've more on my plate than I care to share. I realize you have, too. But bringing her here didn't solve any problems it just made more. We all need to go home and get some rest."

"Charlotte, did I know you had a baby that he took away from you?" Elizabeth's eyes were red and her nose was running. Charlotte was digging in her own pocket and produced a wrinkled tissue.

Shocked, she stared first at her mother and then Jacob. "What have you told her?" Her voice rose. "You are the most ridiculous man on earth to bring this kind of information to her at this stage of her life."

As if defending himself, Jacob held his hand s up. "It wasn't me."

"Then who?" Charlotte's look relayed she wasn't buying that answer.

"Ask her?"

"Mother?"

"Someone called me, said did I know my granddaughter was not too far away from me?" She sobbed into the tissue, which was poor coverage for such heaving. "I asked him and he said its true and she's sick and needs surgery."

Charlotte clutched Jacob's arm. "Is this true?" Her face had turned white. "Why would you tell her and not me?"

"I thought she'd forget it and as you said, she was persistent and I thought," he huffed hot air, rolling his eyes and looking to heaven for help, "like you, I thought it would hush her up. But she's lucid."

"Is Macie sick?" He nodded. "I want to see her."

"No, you agreed. You signed papers."

"Years ago," she replied, bitter, "but that's over. I will take you to court and this time I'll win."

"Join the crowd," he scoffed, sarcastic. "What's one more on my back? Get yourself a lawyer. Get me one." He noticed she was digging in her pocket again and produced her cell. She handed it to him.

"Call Lonnie, tell him you'll be staying with Mrs. Granger tonight. She 's upset and you're settling her down."

"Macie won't accept you."

"You better pray she does, because I'm going to be visible, in fact right there daily in her life whether you like it or not."

"Sounds like I'm going away. I won't be there." Sadness tinged every word. "Not my choice," he finished.

"That is all the more reason for me to be there." She eyed him with contempt. "And don't go worrying how Macie will accept me. She knows my heart beat, and she will remember my arms holding her. She may resist in the beginning but I guarantee you she will come into my arms and I will love her and she will love me."

"Mother's taken good care of her. She's never been without love." His hostility was full blown.

"Get in the vehicle, Jacob. You can tell me what you want, the rest I'll learn as we go along."

A grown man he was thinking, taking orders from an ex wife. He was so weary he text a message to Lonnie, crawled into the Navigator and slumped against the seat defeated but sated. His head was pounding something terrible 'til he thought he'd throw up; served her right if he was sick in her vehicle. Lord, help me he prayed, the pain settling between his eyes as his thoughts went towards Macie. Maybe they'd come to this point for a reason.

His own mother had prayed for years he'd reconcile with Charlotte. He could hear her voice ringing in his ears. "It's not right, Jacob, keeping our sweet girl from her mother. What with my age and your dad's, if something happened to us and even you, who would take our sweet girl?" And as the years passed, she'd remind him "I'm not getting younger, Jacob and you're not getting better, those headaches coming closer and more intense. Contact Charlotte; let her visit Macie before the child gets older and resentful of the situation. She might blame you, robbing her of her mother in her life."

He leaned forward, head in hands the pain throbbing until he could hardly stand it. Now the throbbing robbed him of clear thinking, it was making his body shake. He had no lawyer. If the court appointed one, it would be some underling who had tried few cases. Even if they selected one from Maryville with its larger population it would be pro bono, and who knew where he fit in with other cases?

Who was pressing charges? It was Charlotte's place to do so and he'd not heard she was the one. If it was Raymond, what right did he have? Where did Raymond fit in this comedy? He sobered. If it were Macie, he couldn't stand it, but it was Charlotte and Jack's Lily and that didn't make it much better. Oh, Lord, he prayed, deliver me from this pain, set me on the straight path of thinking and help me when my hands are tied and it seems there's little I can do. Be with my little girl. Be with Macie.

From the visor mirror, Charlotte saw his movement, the pain written on his face. Even in the shadows she saw his body shake. Between Jacob in the back seat and her mother almost abnormally quiet in the front she could only imagine what the rest of the night held. Perhaps by some strike of fate or the power of Jesus, the two would succumb to their body's tiredness and let them all sleep. She must lock the doors and secure the alarm in case her mother wandered. She likened it to the throes of a family death except perhaps worse, these were people very much alive working out their own sufferings. She was a mere by stander whose heart was aching in new realization, she had lost Lily but Macie was near.

She yearned for happy days; days of sunshine and gladness, laughter not sadness and her daughter's smile upon her face. How much gloom could one heart take? Where was her mother's dementia taking her? What was her responsibility to Jacob now that he had reappeared in her life? She had thought she owed him nothing but the years of resentment and hostility that had poisoned her as Jack said and she finally realized she must put it to bed, but now it had resurrected and she, a believer, must handle this situation as a born again follower of Christ was supposed to while her very being rebelled.

She pulled into the drive, hit the button to raise the garage door and they were home. "Mother, we're here. Go in and get ready for bed." She glanced back at Jacob. "Do you need to shower, Jacob? You have the guest room, there's Jack's sweats on the end of the bed. I hope you rest. Goodnight."

No questions? She was letting the interrogation ride? Jacob climbed out of the vehicle, found himself in side, where he removed his shoes at the door and went on down the hall. A shower might help and the pills in his pocket the doctor said he must keep with him at all times. "Thank you," he said, to Charlotte.

* * *

It was a three ring circus. Troy watched the proceedings from his station facing the court room. From the front of the room directly behind the recorder's desk he could watch the Judge, the Sheriff and the Prosecuting Attorney. He wanted to check his watch but no way would he let Wade Bradford sense his concern Jacob would appear on time. He had a feeling of dread on how these proceedings would go. Wade was strutting his stuff. He felt this was his territory and he owned this Court House.

There was a bit of a hustle at the door. Maryville's own Daily Press had received news of the days happening and was present just outside the courtroom door. He heard voices and knew Jacob had arrived. But to his surprise, Jacob was not alone. Charlotte was in tow of a very well dressed Jacob, her mother and a distinguished looking gentleman Troy did not know.

Across the room, Wade Bradford took notice. He bent to speak with the Prosecuting Attorney. Three seats from the front, Raymond Long sat up straighter as if a mighty hand had reached down and raised him full height in his chair. His countenance dropped a mark or two and Troy could see his curiosity was peaked.

The Court Bailiff came from the back room. "All please stand. This Court of Sand County in the city of Maryville, and the state of Missouri is now in session, The Honorable Dred L Collier presiding.

Langston Collier, as Troy knew him, took his seat. Rapped twice with the gavel and said "all be seated." There was the usual shuffle, a cough or two as the Judge continued, "The Case against Jacob Long by Sand County authorities shall come to order. Prosecuting Attorney A.T. Atwell, you may present."

Dred L. Collier owned the Court Room, not Wade Bradford or any other counselor. If he deemed it his right to proceed according to his own jurisdiction, he did so. No one bucked him. Troy rather enjoyed watching his school friend perform. Many a side wink had been cast his direction. Wade Bradford might have the Prosecuting Attorney in his pocket but he doubted anyone owned Dred L. Collier, and yet the man m ust make his decisions according to the law and he was a stickler for that. However, he would tell you, the fate of the one standing before him was not in his hands but in the ability and skill of one's own lawyer, whether he had done his home work and spoke for you or had failed in that first step of your hiring.

The Bailiff collected the papers from the prosecuting attorney and handed them to the Judge.

"Good morning, Your Honor. This is an arraignment," A.T. Atwell said, as he approached the bench. "The Court has an eye witness that Jacob Long was present the night little Lily Delang was found dead on the bench on Hwy 21, near the city entrance to Perish, Missouri on the fifteenth day of May, twenty eighteen."

"It is our firm belief for the sake of society that Jacob Long not be allowed bail but this day be admitted to the Sand County Jail Facility at Greenway."

"Does the offender have counsel?"

A.T. Atwell turned to study the empty chairs around the table where Jacob was sitting. "I'm not aware, Your Honor."

"Will counsel for and Mr. Long please approach the bench?"

Jacob rose and turned toward the area where Charlotte and the stranger were sitting. The gentleman arose, tipped his head to Jacob and joined him to walk the few steps forward. He spoke with the Baliff briefly and was presented to the court as Clayton John Demaree legal defense representation for Jacob Long.

In the remaining hour, the Honorable Dred L Collier denied the States request for immediate incarceration, appointed Charlotte Delang as friend of the Court, something not used in Maryville's system in years and became the brunt end of the case.

Tongue in cheek, Troy Sanders watched Wade Bradford. It was clear; he was not satisfied at all with the Judge's decision that Jacob Long was released into Charlotte's custody. It was unheard of, Friend of the Court was used in situations of children needing someone to watch out for them, but a grown man? Almost, Troy smiled. He heard the discussion. Dred Langston Collier, the Honorable Judge did not say specifically Friend of the Court, he said in comparison to he would release Jacob due to circumstance in which the mother of the child was present and appeared by her own words not to blame Jacob Long, her ex-husband, for the child's death. Dred L. Collier probably wished to throw the whole thing out, but with Wade Bradford and A.T. Atwell running hot in the next election he decided to help them out.

Sometimes it all came down to you scratch my back and I'll scratch yours.

Now, Troy's attention shifted to Charlotte. She had dressed Jacob up. No doubt he was wearing her husband's clothes and they fit well. It was good Jacob had liked Jack Delang, otherwise he might feel resentful. Studying Jacob, Troy saw the wheels of the man's frustration working in the expression on his face. Almost, one could laugh, fate had a way of settling a man down to what the facts of life really were, you have no control over anything when you most need it. Like it or not, Jacob was in Charlotte's clutches for the time being and Troy doubted even the Honorable Judge had an inkling of what he had done. All these years, ignoring the needs of Macie, Jacob now must face Charlotte's reentry into the life of their child.

It was a sobering thought, made Troy want to consider his own life. Why had he gone into law enforcement? Because he thought the underdog deserved a chance and there were always men like Oscar and Raymond ready to take advantage of the less fortunate. What trait of the character would you label that? Greed, he surmised and decided in his position few opportunities to be greedy would present themselves and that was a good thing. He was a working man, a God fearing believer that he had better live right or God would allow someone else his job. Well, the courtroom was cleared. He followed the last person out as Dred reappeared from the back, lift a hand in a wave and got into his car.

* * *

Bewildered, Jacob stood mute, staring across the Courtyard Square of Sand County. His new lawyer, Clayton John Demaree, by his side, waited for his client to speak. Stubborn, obstinate as a little boy found with his hand in the cookie jar, Jacob felt he could out last the man.

"Your thoughts?" Demaree asked. Charlotte had called him, questioning his opinion of the case against her former husband. "Do you think he is guilty?" His one question and her answer decided the issue. He hopped the first plane from Washington, D.C., to this forsaken little berg of a town, to face the scrutiny of townsfolk who probably resented a city slicker as one person at the hotel labeled him when he checked in. They were a people a bit rough around the edges, he decided, but mostly good folks, the kind his family came from, working people scrounging out a living with the best intentions and a lot of struggle.

"Don't make your impression of us, based on this town," the old fellow at the gas pump had said, when he asked, "how does the population of Maryville make a living? Thus far, I've seen nothing but rolling hills and countryside filled with a few wandering cattle. What lies beyond this Courtyard town?"

"There's farm land worth the mint," the old man replied."Those who own, got it made, those who don't have to look elsewhere. They go to the city. But," he had paused, thinking, "lot of them return. There really is no place like home and this is where their heart is, a slower pace, a more gentle life. How's yours?"

Charlotte was headed his way. Jacob Long had not replied. How do you work with a man who won't speak? He wondered, but Charlotte said not to worry. Jacob Long had far more to gain than lose, strange words, Clayton surmised, from what he received of the story in that one telephone conversation. His client was blamed for death of Charlotte's child, which she said was impossible, he also had a daughter of his own very ill, Charlotte implied needed him present for an important surgery. Well, Jack Delang saved his life, it was the least he could do to help Charlotte with this strange situation.

He reviewed their conversation as she approached, "Charlotte," he asked when she called, "what state are you in?" He had to think a moment. "Yes, I did handle that case in St. Louis. We are all right, Charlotte. If there's a problem with the Court Magistrate, I'm sure there will be time before the trial to obtain the necessary license but I believe pro hac vice is a clause will come in to play, which is a limited license provided by your court system."

* * *

Charlotte's insides were churning. On the outside, she must appear calm and as though she knew the outcome of this present day trial would be victorious, but inside she had to draw on the strength that came only from the Lord, for by herself she would fail. Sometimes, in the night she awakened to fears overwhelming, questions that provoked an unrest only her faith in God would quell.

Who could imagine? Had she not prayed for years God would allow the return of Macie? Lily had filled the emptiness of her arms, for a time and then Lily was gone. One friend had written in a card I know your loss has shaken the very foundation of your belief, Charlotte, but you must not allow the devil to take control for he is standing there waiting to destroy your salvation and make you as the next person who has lost all hope.

It was true, as her friend said, she could become a crumbled heap of humanity lying on the floor grieving the loss of Lily's life, the terrible acceptance that beautiful little girl was gone and once more her arms were empty, she must deal with her mother's dementia and even the knowledge her ex-huband was once more nearby to create further havoc and chaos in her life, here in her own home?

How could she be involved in saving him from another prison sentence? Would they ever know what happened with Lily? The Coroner said, "there are no broken bones, Charlotte. Lily was not hit by an automobile, if anything she died instantly almost as though she was drugged but what we will never understand, the most confusing of circumstance is how did Lily come to life's end on that forsaken bench near the entrance to our city? I have one more test to run and then perhaps we will know."

They had returned from the Court Proceedings, Jacob taking residence in the room down the hall. Her mother's dementia seemed on hold, and that was a mystery to Charlotte. There, but for the grace of God, go I, she thought. Surely the prayers of her friends had something to do with her mother's calm. When she considered the turmoil of that rainy night, the house in the woods, it all seemed a story someone concocted from thin air, no one experienced such unbelievable events in real life, but she did.

She arose early, thinking to prepare for the day before the other two, but no, Jacob was in the kitchen. He nodded his countenance aloof, his eyes disdainful of her hold on him. "Good morning," she said. He didn't reply. "I know you aren't happy with this change of events," she said, "but try to put aside yesterday's fiasco and let us decide what to do about Macie. Today, I expect to be reunited with my child. I want to know exactly what is needed and whether the doctor will see if I'm a match for her kidney transplant."

"I won't be part of that," he replied. "She is not well. You can't just march in and say, hello, Macie, I'm your mother." He ladled scrambled eggs onto two plates, the usual strips of bacon and waited for the toaster to produce beautifully tanned bread. "I've searched for the jelly and can't find it."

"Sometimes Mother puts it in the pantry, not the refrigerator," she said, opening the pantry door. "yes." The phone rang as she set the jelly on the table and answered the phone to listen and then comment on the call. "The lawn service cannot come until next week. I only hired them because of mother's wanderings, I suppose I shall handle that little chore myself since she seems to have settled down."

Jacob dismissed Charlotte's domestic problem. "You are too old; your organ would undoubtedly be too large for a child as frail as Macie."

"Let the doctor be the judge of that. If there's no one else and she is as seriously ill as you imply then there's every reason to at least pursue the matter. You don't have the final say in this, Jacob."

Their eyes met, steeled against further words or emotion, one would not bow to the other but common sense said they must give up their differences for the need of their child. That he denied her admittance to Macie was no longer a concern to Charlotte. "What time shall we leave for your parent's home?"

"No." He stared at her. "We will see the doctor first, no false hopes for any of us, then we will decide about Macie. I don't know how to introduce you. This is something I've never considered…you knowing my daughter."

"Almost, I find that comment ridiculous." Her eyes were pin points. "Your daughter," she said sarcastically. "I'll let it ride. You have no choice in this new journey of our daughter's life." How easily she had fallen into the same old trap, caution to the wind and disparaging words between them. "I suggest you call Macie's doctor as soon as the office opens. I can leave within fifteen minutes of knowing."

Love does not rejoice in iniquity, but rejoices in truth

Chapter 9

As before, Jacob cleared the kitchen, leaving a plate for Elizabeth on the table. From the window he saw Charlotte going through the motions of mowing the lawn. Life had its ironies, the mundane needs of life were carried out on a simple basis while the ultimate battles were subject to wait. He made the call to Macie's doctor. "It's not questionable," the doctor replied, " time is of the essence. I will make room for a consultation with this new donor possibility. Shall we set the appointment for one o'clock?"

Jacob had not told Dr. Cameron the new donor was Macie's mother. As far as he knew her mother was dead. Going out to face Charlotte, Jacob saw she was not moving across the lawn as intended but had the lawn mower in a precarious position where the lawn met the city's drain pipe. She was trying in vain to back the mower out of that dangerous spot but her weight was not enough to do so. Without a word, Jacob stepped on to the back bar of the mower and Charlotte pulled away.

"You have an appointment?" He nodded. "After lunch," she asked.

"One o'clock," Jacob replied, and turned to walk back to the house. He had seen the pile of clothes she had deposited by the bedroom door. That they were once Jack's clothing did not bother him. He dressed carefully, realizing no request was too much in the event the judicial system inspected his clothing. But this was Macie's doctor's office they would visit. Shoes were available but no socks. He sit down to wait for Charlotte, wondering that Elizabeth had not yet made an appearance for the day.

Charlotte finished the mowing and returned to the house. She saw him sitting on the steps to the stair that led up to her mother's room. "Has she stirred?" She asked. He shook his head. "No worry," she said noticing the shoes and his bare feet. "You know where my room is; Jack's socks are still in the corner chest of drawers. Find whatever you need." That was Charlotte, let others do something for themselves otherwise the task would be hers and she had enough on her plate as the old saying went. He found the piece of furniture and knew she had entered the room behind him. He heard the shower running and made himself finish the task he had previously begun, dressing in the clothes she laid out, finally examining his image in the long wall mirror.

It seemed Jack's clothing fit him, he could only imagine what others would think if they knew he was wearing her late husband's clothing. The truth was that he and Jack Delang held much in common. He didn't mind wearing Jack's clothes. They had shared the same woman, no doubt understanding Charlotte was an exceptional being, but he was responsible for sharpening her need to think things through, to understand all people were not good, nor kind, nor respectful. That was what he taught her. Possibly, Jack taught her how to deal with people such as the Jacob Longs of the world.

Charlotte was a beautiful woman. She dressed in a classic style, her wardrobe was not filled to capacity, instead an array of possibly twenty pieces hung from the racks though there were more in the long dresser of her closet. Shoes and handbags were a subdued hue of taupe, grays and black. She learned to add color with the scarf or chosen piece of jewelry. Jacob knew she would not have changed from the woman he married nor through her high profile husband Jack Delang's ministering to Washington's elite. She was born a lady but the edge of gentleness seemed to have been replaced by a hard edge, whether his or Jack Delang's fault.

Again he sat waiting on the stair steps, his eyes straying to the photos on the living room's fireplace mantle. Lily smiled a seven year old toothless grin, changing in the next photo to a more serious eight year old, the photos progressing as each year of life unfolded; down to the one he believed her last, a close up of her eyes, heavily fringed with black lashes, a hint of a smile shadowing her lips and the jolt of reality hit him.

For a moment his chest seemed to contract the breath squeezed out of him as he clutched the rail. Lily could have been Macie at age seven. Had there been a time he and Charlotte were together before he took Macie away? Yes, yes, there was. His chest tightened and for a moment he had difficulty breathing deep. Of course the two girls would look alike, Charlotte was their mother, but he had been told by many that Macie resembled him.

"Ready?" Charlotte slung a small purse across her left shoulder, picked up the keys off the center cabinet and led the way to the Navigator. "I had the neighbor's son freshen the vehicle. Are you comfortable riding shotgun or do you wish to sit in the back?"

"Here's fine," he replied, wondering that she even offered him the courtesy. "What about your mother?"

She gave him a curious glance. "Mother isn't even up. She does this, when overly tired and then rested up she has the energy of an eighteen year old. So, of course, she won't be going with us. The neighbor is there in case Mother needs something."

"Are you trying to be nice, Charlotte?"

"I will do anything for Macie."

* * *

Dr. Cameron had been part of the study three years now. His interest was not only in the success of the study but the individual, whether child or adult. That Jacob Long was bringing a possible donor for his daughter was interesting. Having read the latest flash of newspaper articles on the once famous ball player, he could only wonder if this would prove another disappointment to father and child.

The father and possible donor were shown into his personal office. "You are?" He addressed Charlotte Delang.

"Family relation," Jacob Long replied.

"We have this form for you to fill in the blanks," Dr. Cameron was saying, noting the woman's composure and the intensity he felt from the handshake to being seated and listening wide eyed as he explained the procedure.

"Mr. Long expressed concern, an adult donor for a child but we do have studies to prove survival rates. Of course, best results happen when the donor is one of the children's parents which then presents a new challenge of keeping the kidney functioning after what appears a successful transfer of the kidney to the recipient."

"If you continue in this effort we will begin with a twenty four hour urine sample to examine the function of your kidney. There will be a blood test to first identify your blood type and determine if the two of you are compatible."

"How does that work?"

"Blood cells from both of you are mixed. If Macie's cells destroy the donor cells it is positive and we cannot use your kidney. This means there are antibodies present and Macie's body would put up a fight to destroy the kidney. If the cross match is negative, Macie does not have antibodies against your donor kidney and we can proceed with plans for surgery. We hope for a high Antigen match. If there's a match, you will have a chest x-ray and an EKG." The doctor glanced away, studying the photo behind a glass cabinet of his own daughter, age twelve. She ran and played continuously but what he realized in Macie Long's case was a dwindling energy level. "Should all test prove a positive match between the two of you we will do surgery within the day because we have cleared Macie for this surgery previously.

"Will the test be out-patient?"

Dr. Cameron studied the two. They had not revealed their connection. However he detected a form of hostility between them. Feuding family, he surmised when he wished for Macie's sake, the woman was her mother. Wearily he wiped a hand across his face. "Would it be asking too much of you to stay within our facilities confines? Once a donor is found, that cuts down on the issue of unexpected accident and perhaps even encountering sickness of one sort or another."

"Whatever Macie needs, I am happy to comply," Mrs. Delang replied.

"I believe you will be quite comfortable."

Jacob was noncommittal. By now, he should be accustomed to people in high places making demands, doing what they thought best when really it was one man's guess as good as the next. They were led to a studio apartment with a small kitchenette, the living area complete with a television and a sleeping area that revealed two regular sized beds. He checked the closet; pajamas for each and a robe, a plastic container in the robe pocket revealed hygienic items, a toothbrush, toothpaste, body wash, and deodorant.

"Unbelievable," he muttered. "It is almost as though we are prisoners." He gave a deep sigh. "I thought we would be visiting my parents this night, instead, look at us. I don't buy this and maybe you shouldn't either."

"We have nothing to lose and everything to gain," she replied. "I don't care that the doctor asked us to stay. So he's a bit eccentric. Remember the officials we have encountered dealing with Lily's death?" Taking a plush afghan from one end of the sofa she draped it around her shoulders. "Perish is filled with some strange characters. I wonder if it's the town's history pulls them in?"

There was a knock at the door and a girl pushed a white clothed server into the room. She stopped at the small glass topped table, deposited the two dome covered plates, lay the silverware, checked the server of its remaining contents and left.

"I thought we'd been bad and were being sent to bed without dinner," Jacob quipped. "Bon appetite." The food was tasty. A small sirloin steak, a baked potato and a Caesar salad did ease their hunger.

She stifled a yawn behind her hand. "I didn't sleep well, last night. I think I'll retire." Her eyes were on the plastic container the nurse gave her. "As you said, life is a hoot. Maybe one day the memory from tonight will be worth remembering."

"Somehow, right now I have doubts," he replied. "I'm headed for bed, too. My head throbs and I'm tired to the bone. He would not admit his conscience held a nagging secret that worried him considerably.

"This is plain scary," Charlotte whispered. "Do you think the room is bugged?"

Jacob began to laugh. "I'm sorry, Charlotte, but that's an understatement. I think this little safe harbor is a rich man's toy? Meaning, the good doctor wants to see the reaction of those who enter?"

"And you are not afraid?" She persisted.

"Not if it doesn't get any worse than this." He was loosening the belt to his pants; she turned aside while he laid them on a chair, omitted the pajamas in the closet and slid into bed. Charlotte, on the other hand stepped inside the closet, found her personal stack and put on the provided pajamas.

"Charlotte," Jacob raised his voice to reach her. "Do you remember the time your dad was in Mercy Hospital? It was nothing but empty beds where they took us, the night they ask if we would be so kind to stay close by and would we consider sleeping on fifth floor in their Family Unit." His chuckle was good natured. "It was family oriented, all right. All those other couples, sleeping on those reserved hospital beds. And that one amorous young couple…."

"It was their Honeymoon, Jacob." She tried to sound restricting but the memory was strong and she began to laugh, a strange hollow sound that evolved into nervous giggles."I can't believe I'm laughing," she said. "Goodnight, Jacob."

"Good night, Charlotte." As simple as that he said goodnight, when he wanted to ask her, was Lily my child?

* * *

The good doctor stood at the door. His intention was to tell them results to the first test but hearing they were retiring for the night, his hand stopped mid-air before the knock. Had he detect a loosening of the hostility perhaps in laughter? He hoped for Macie's sake. Sighing, he walked away. His own family was waiting at home. Sometimes it was difficult deciding where he was most needed. For now, a smile appeared in his heart. "yes," he said softly, "laughter is the best medicine."

* * *

Charlotte's nervousness explained the laughter. She had succumbed to the giggles much as a teenage girl. Whatever tomorrow would bring, she prayed for Macie. Her prayer progressed to the part of forgiveness and there she found herself caught between earth's practicality and Heaven's expectations. Why wouldn't she hold Jacob responsible for losing her daughter? Hadn't she tried through the years to loosen that hold, bring suit against him and retrieve her child? Years of effort merely revealed the power behind the written agreement she signed in order to save her own sanity and then to mother Lily as her second daughter deserved.

Yawning, she slid deeper into the sheets, hearing Jacob's even breathing. How strange to be lying in a room near a man she harbored contempt for all these years, to hear a catch to his breathing now and then and realize he was not without pain, the pills merely dulled it. What was God telling her? Let go. Your feelings of the past have nothing to do with now. But she had nursed them as one would until they were engrained, a part of her as much as the fingers on her hand, fine tuned that dreadful hurt of losing Macie always rose up. Let me hold this much, the injustice was too great? I cannot forgive this man. If you do not forgive, then how can I forgive you? Was God speaking to her consciousness?

Turning on her side she tried to sleep. I am waiting, Charlotte. Was God really waiting? She could not turn loose. Charlotte, we must work together, the three of us, do you want to jeopardize the days ahead by your own stubbornness? She sighed. What do you want? Turn loose. The battle is not won. You will need to ask my intervention in the days to come, Macie will have her moments. Did she imagine she heard a slight chuckle? Was God really laughing? Your daughter formed by my participation carries within her a form of stubbornness equal to her parents. Now, go to sleep, Charlotte, the road ahead is not without risk…but I will be with you to the end.

Charlotte awakened to sunlight streaming through the opened blinds. It was morning. She had slept. An urgent need bloomed in her mind, sped to her heart and caused her to reach for the small drawer centered in the bedside table. Inside she found a bible and allowed it to spill open. 1 Corinthians 2:9, she read, "But as it is written, eye hath not seen, nor ear heard, neither have entered into the heart of man the things which God hath prepared for them that love him."

Jacob turned and saw her expression. It was priceless. One thing they shared, loving God and knowing he loved them. It was their ways threatened the peace God offered. Jacob sat down on the bed, took the Bible from Charlotte's hand and read. "Eye hath not seen nor ear heard neither have entered in to the heart of man the things which God hath prepared for them that love him."

Rising, he stared down on this woman who had once been his wife. "I'm game, if you are."

"Give up years of thinking one way?" She groped for words to explain. None came.

"If you think about it, Charlotte, you won't do it, if you let go and let God you can do it."

* * *

Charlotte showered and dressed in yesterday's clothes. Returning to the living area she found Jacob studying the white clothed cart that had been brought in with breakfast dishes. "It was almost as though I thought it and this food appeared." Chagrined, Jacob shook his head. "Sometimes the things rich people are capable of, scares me and I'm not easily scared."

"No," she agreed, "Because you are one of them."

"Somehow it's not the same when you can't get your hands on your own possessions," he replied. "You seemed to have slept well last night."

"And you?" She questioned.

"Actually, I was surprised that I did. Now, if today will bring good news for Macie..." The phone rang as he spoke and Jacob answered. "Yes, certainly, in one hour. We will be there." Lifting the domed lid from one of the dishes, he glanced up. "The test results concerning your compatibility to Macie are in."

"Are they compatible?"

"We will learn that from the good doctor in one hour. Have breakfast, his Nurse said and then come on down."

"I was thinking, if we were asked to stay last night, what about the next days if there's a match."

"Yeah, I thought of that, too," Jacob replied, dishing scrambled eggs onto his plate. "That would mean they would bring Macie in and of course, Mom and Pop. They're rather tied up in Macie."

A sad smile hovered on Charlotte's face. "I always regretted our being forced to drop our relationship. Your parents were good people and I appreciated them, but how they will feel about me now..." She let the words drop.

"Don't worry about that, Mom made it quite clear you got the bad end of the deal." He sighed. "But you are right, now could be different. You are now a threat to their number one position as Macie's care givers." He watched her nibble at a piece of bacon. "There's fruit? Pineapple and peach, kind of a strange mix."

"Suddenly," she said, "My stomach is tied in knots. I don't think I better eat anything fresh. In fact, maybe nothing for now until we hear what the doctor has to say." She rinsed her hands at the sink and went to the sofa. "I'm sure my nerves will collapse by the end of day."

"I've thought on this, Charlotte, if the report is positive, not meaning the medical term of possible rejection but in this case the advancement toward surgery, I will introduce you to Macie as a nice lady willing to contribute a kidney." He paused to stare at the table. "I honestly don't know what the best way to handle this is." He was still reeling from things he should have known but refused to see.

Tears welled up in Charlotte's eyes. "I'm blessed to think of that possibility." For a minute she was vulnerable to his usual sarcasm but for some reason he glanced away as if he didn't notice.

"When you're ready, I think we should go and sit in the doctor's waiting room." Nervous, he jingled the coins in his pant pocket. "I would have preferred we hear this a month earlier before Macie became so frail and now she has a lot to deal with."

"Of course you mean me." Charlotte was overwhelmed. Her body sagged in despair. Words without meaning attacked her; she had kept her chin up, she had broad shoulders, sticks and stones might break her bones… but yes, words did hurt her. Her mind was racing here and there, trying to think what if she was not a match, what if she was? She felt as though she was coming unglued. It was all too much. She had made it through losing Lily with the help of five little girls. Much as she disliked admitting it, Jacob helped with her mother in the woods. Who was going to help her now? For a moment, time was swirling around her, she was caught in a wind, nothing was balanced, nothing was sane, the last six months whirled faster and faster…she had to get off…she had to get off… she had to…she had…she…she felt herself crumbling….

"Charlotte, are you all right?" Jacob's hand was on her arm, she was leaning against the wall. "This is not like you, Charlotte. I thought I heard you moan." He was peering into her face, his expression one of complete desolation. "I'd say anxiety almost got you. Think nothing of it. I've been there, done that."

It was that moment, Charlotte realized, she would accept the task that lay before her, whether she was a donor or taking on the role of mother to a little girl who would need someone with her through every trial her issue of health might bring. This moment, she whispered. "This moment." She wiped her face, wiped away the fear and despair, wiped away the devil's hold on her mind. "I am a child of the King," she whispered. "No weapon formed against me shall prosper, every tongue which rises against me in judgment God will condemn. This is the heritage of the servants of the Lord; My righteousness is from Him, says the Lord."

"Isaiah fifty four. Seventeen," Jacob quoted. "I learned that through Jack when my future seemed black. Did you know he visited me? I can still hear his voice, "Take heed, Brother," he said. "God is not mocked. He wants good for us, Jacob, not bad. Our God is a positive God and we are his children."

Charlotte gave an embarrassed laugh. "I don't know what came over me, deep thoughts I guess. I felt myself spinning and these crazy words circling my head. But it was real, wasn't it? I don't know what to say."

"You don't have to explain, Charlotte. Whether the doctor tells us everything is a match or not, you are willing to put your life on the line for Macie." His voice dropped lower. "I've suffered times of complete denial of what was happening to me, and rallied to know life hits hard, it is my cross…"

"Mr. Long. Mrs. Delang." Dr. Cameron's nurse held the door for their entrance in to Dr. Cameron's office once more. Sitting behind his desk studying papers, he motioned for them to be seated.

"Thus far, things are looking good," he said. "The blood test is a match, the tissue typing is perfect, Mrs. Delang as if you were Macie's mother. We could not ask for a better Antigen count." He lift his eyes to Charlotte, "It is almost as though all your markers are the same, Mrs. Delang. How could that be?"

"I am Macie's birth mother."

"Ahh, as I hoped but you gave me nothing to go on." Now he tilt his head, waiting for more information.

"Macie does not know me. She was taken from me while an infant."

"Then you have reappeared in her life at a most opportune time." He said gently. "Do not fret, Mrs. Delang, God is in control. I believe that as surely as I am now sitting in front of this desk. It is fact." He cast his eyes on Jacob Long, there was no accusing factor only satisfaction in two parents doing as they should to prolong the life of their child.

"The question on my mind," Jacob said, "is how Macie will emotionally accept the fact her mother is now in her life. Do you have advice as to how we should handle that part of the equation?"

"What is an equation?" Dr. Cameron stared out the window. "An equation is the process of associating one thing to another." He had asked for a view of the rolling hill, no parking lot, only God's green earth, the blue sky and a possibility of a flying bird or a butterfly to confront his mind when there were the usual frailties of human choices pressed upon him. "An equation always has an answer but sometimes it may be what we least expect. Why don't you put that in the hands of one far wiser than this doctor?"

* * *

This was it. Charlotte's emotions were over the top. She had not met her daughter and here they were ready for a surgery the doctor said could last four to however many hours necessary, and when Jacob pressed Dr. Cameron said probably eight but maybe nine hours, resisting unexpected happenings he hoped the less hours for Macie to be asleep, considering her frail condition.

They came in to administer the intravenous procedure necessary for the surgery.

She had tried to listen, keep her mind neutral to the fact this was her body, she was losing a kidney, the recipient, as Macie was called, was her daughter. There she lost all neutrality. This was her child. Flesh of flesh, taken from her body, eleven years ago and ripped from her arms ten of those last years.

Breathe. Breathe. Keep the blood pressure level. Breathe. They would begin soon. The kidney would be removed from her body, barring complications, and transferred to Macie's. "It is a matter of beginning the attachment of the new kidney's blood vessels to Macie's," Dr. Cameron explained. "This being a live transplant there will be two teams, one for Mrs. Delang and the other for Macie." At that point Dr. Cameron became silent, studying her for a time before he continued. "If, you decide the procedure too much for you, at any time, up to the moment of surgery you may change your mind."

That statement being said, the doctor moved on, "When all goes well, as planned, the donor stays in the hospital two or three days according to their need and then we ask that you remain near the clinic an additional week after your discharge."

"You will need someone with you who takes your needs to heart and desires to help you through this time of healing. It is not a cold hearted wish of our team to monitor your health but a desire to help the next patient who will travel this road."

It was at that moment she saw in Dr. Cameron the weariness of having lost a patient perhaps in the past and his determination to have the best team members. No doubt he hand selected them in the beginning until he realized his own zeal would lose effect if he was worn thin from the process. His calling as surgeon, in his mind, was ordained by the one on high who made all things possible.

"Your surgery will be done using a procedure we call laparoscopic nephrectomy." He continued. "This procedure is performed under general anesthesia and uses a smaller incision, much like you may have heard used in the removal of a gall bladder. A camera views inside your body and tells the surgeon what to do with his magic wand of retrieval and your hospital stay will be remarkably shorter and your healing time of recovery even better than the older practice of open surgery."

"You are thinking again. I recognize that look." Jacob stood by her bed. "They will be taking you soon. I was advised to come and kiss you before surgery." He gave an embarrassed laugh. "Somehow, they are so tied up in the fact I am Macie's father and you are her mother, they are missing the difference in names. I suppose the world waits for a love story." He placed her hand in his.

She smiled, whether the drugs or her own desire to go into this surgery with a mind cleared of old resentment and blame toward Jacob, she didn't know, but she felt the smile, gentle on her face. He leaned across the tangle of tubes and placed his lips on hers. "For old times' sake, Charlotte, God bless you through this time of giving. I am most grateful."

She could wallow in the past or go forward into the future. She chose the latter. The psychologist had met with her. "We do not know what your child will do, learning you are her birth mother. You are doing all in your power to lengthen her life, but will she waste time wondering why you abandoned her?" She put her hand up, "yes, I know, the father took her… but Macie does not understand that part of life. She will learn of it in the future. You must be strong, Mrs. Delang. That is your next task."

* * *

The last thing she remembered was Jacob's eyes kind, for a change. They were giving each other the benefit of the doubt; they could start over for Macie. But how would Macie feel knowing her mother was alive and had been all along?"

"Mrs. Long?" She felt someone patting her face. "Mrs. Long. Time to wake up."

Sleep felt good. Charlotte ignored the nurse. It was a dream. "Mrs. Long?"

She heard a chuckle, joined by another. "You try. Sometimes a familiar voice is needed."

"I don't know about familiar," Jacob replied. "Charlotte, do you want to know how things are going with our daughter?" The soft laughter continued. "Charlotte, they are almost finished with Macie."

"Macie?" She brought a hand from under the sheet. Searching the bed beside her she found nothing.

"Charlotte, your hands are cold." Jacob's voice held a hint of humor. "Cold hands warm heart, or is it cold heart, Charlotte?" His voice low, he said, "Charlotte, remember that trip to the Gulf Shores when the storm brought the ocean waves lapping at the hotel where we stayed and you ran trying to beat them. We both ran." His chuckle grew, the nurse laughing with him, not because she held the memory but he appeared happy in the retelling to his wife. "We were so cold; in the middle of August we went to our room and lit a fire in the fireplace. You said, that must happen often, why else would they have a fireplace and wood ready to use. Remember, Charlotte?"

"I remember," she whispered. "You ended up carrying me after I fell and scraped my knee."

"You did fall, didn't you." He glanced at the nurse. "I forgot that part. Heaven yes, I carried you up the stairs to our room because they had stopped the elevators." He grinned. "I believe she's awake."

"Good job," the nurse said. "Now, Mrs. Long, once your good kidney functions on its own we will move you to your room. You have done exceptionally well, my dear and I'm sure your husband will take good care of you."

The nurse bustled out of the room, carrying the excess pads she had removed from Charlotte's bed. Jacob leaned across, his eyes on Charlotte, still holding her hand. "I didn't have the heart to tell her, we are no longer married. Remember what I said, the world wants a love story. We can give them that, Charlotte, a love for our little girl."

"Shame." She searched for words but her mouth was dry and her brain seemed unable to go beyond one word. To speak took every ounce of her energy. She was tired. She would sleep.

"Shame we aren't husband and wife or shame she made the mistake?" Jacob's voice teased.

"That's not…funny," she tried to articulate, but she felt groggy and unsettled. Why was he smiling? "Charlotte, girl, you take me back to when Macie was born, you couldn't talk then either." For all she cared he could shut up. "You were a beautiful mother, Charlotte, so happy. Blessed you said."

Charlotte slept; the dreams parading across the darkness of her mind, on their own they created Jacob rocking Macie, Jacob handing her Macie with poopy diapers, Jacob dancing across the floor with Macie in his arms, laying her in the bed to take Charlotte's hand and lead her across the room as though ball room dancing were his chosen profession. "Aren't you glad our coach makes us dance?" He asked.

She rallied for the nurse, was patient when they took her vitals, grimaced when the cuff grew tight, smiled when they squeezed her finger, but she slept, reliving every day with Jacob, smiling as his eyes lit up seeing Macie and then the darkness filed across her brain, the women who called and asked if he was home, the late nights when he stumbled up the stairs intoxicated to the point of waking the next morning fully clothed, dirt on the bed covers where he had slept in his shoes.

The laughter changed to sobbing, her own frustration. His parent's coming to speak to him, to plead. Then came the terrible accident and the hospital where he rejected her and filed for a divorce. She tried to come out of the darkness; the nurse summoning Jacob. She heard their voices.

"I don't know what's happening to your wife, Mr. Long, whether it is the anesthesia of if I should call the doctor. Do you want to try one more thing before I make that call? Crawl up in the bed, Mr. Long and hold your wife. Help her through this sad time. It is an organ she has given away, but her dreams seem to have become nightmares of a different loss."

* * *

He knew. Jacob listened to her breathing, heard the moans, caught phrases that brought back memory of those last months they shared as husband and wife. The sobbing, yes and the loss. He knew. Without Charlotte he felt he was sinking in those days. Then the accident and she didn't come immediately. He called the lawyer. Do whatever you must to make sure Macie stays with me. But this was a different day. She had given a future to Macie. He held her, whispered in her ear, calmed her and waited for the doctor. The nurse was making the call. "The anesthesiologist thinks it is the drugs," she e said, hoping to ease his concern. "Some people cannot take the steroids, they hallucinate and have nightmares, others react to the anesthesia."

She studied him. He seemed to love her. "What kind of person is your wife?" She asked. "I mean is she a teacher, a leader, a follower, what is her role in life?"

"She's all things," he whispered, ashamed of his role in making the years hard for Charlotte. "She is a teacher, a leader who is willing to follow. She's a lady, a good mother." He did not say, "but I am going to hurt her again."

Love bears all things, believes all things, hopes all things

Chapter 10

Bentley's mother stopped in. "The Nurse almost didn't let me see you. I had to go through fifty questions, have I been well? When was my last cold? Have I been around an infant with measles? The list was pretty long, but I don't mind Charlotte, they are watching out for you."

"I think I'm fine." Charlotte lay a hand on the area she suspected the kidney was removed from. "It's kind of like what people describe as after an appendectomy. I guess I still have mine. But, yeah I'm a little sore and a whole lot apprehensive. You know, meeting Macie after all these years."

"I'm sure that will be good for both of you." She was searching in her purse. "That reminds me, though I don't know why, Julie gave me a note from your mother. She says your mother is lucid, caught up in some new venture up stairs and understands she cannot come to see you, but she thinks of you."

Charlotte grinned. "Maybe she won't try to cook while I'm gone. I don't really trust her in the kitchen, I guess the fear she might go off and leave a burner on and burn the house down." She sighed, wearily. "Thank you, all of you for helping with mother. She's always been such a rock and now this, her failing memory, the trauma of losing Lily and here I am…." Her words trailed off, "how do you suppose she will handle a new granddaughter? Sometimes I think we all have to face a cruel season of life. Mother was so strong, she and dad were pillars of the community, now to face this kind of an end forgetful and even reliving your life on a different level. She loves to have the girls around, and watch them play. I almost wonder if she will lose more ground and become a child again."

"If she does, Charlotte, then let her enjoy, don't be ashamed. The girls love he." Seeing Charlotte's sadness, she thought to change the subject. "How's it going with Jacob?" She lay a folded paper on Charlotte's tray. "There's the letter."

'I'm not certain. He said if the doctor allowed it, once I'm released he will take me to see Macie. But he tends to keep her all to himself, tries to at least…and his parents…I thought they would stop in but they haven't so I suppose all the old guide lines are still in play."

"In just the short time you've kept Jacob under foot, we all discussed this, that he looks better and actually performs as a real person, some of his old hang ups nearly did us In, but he's more human, not as sarcastic as previous to Macie's surgery and yours. You look good, Charlotte, ready to leave here."

Charlotte glanced around the room, "I'm ready to see my child, but I have to stay close to the doctors for a week, and then I'll be home to take care of mother."

The next day brought unexpected pain to Charlotte. "My stomach feels like it's on fire," she said to the nurse on duty that morning. "And my leg feels like it weighs a ton. Should I get up and walk the kinks out?"

"Let's run a simple test," the doctor said when he was summoned and late that afternoon, he returned, a frown on his brow. "It seems you have developed a blood clot. We are already on it. Just stay calm and let the meds dissolve that pesky little fellow and then you will be out of here." He tried to smile.

"Is something bothering you, Dr. Cameron? You don't seem yourself."

"I believe I'm preoccupied, Mrs. Delang, but I can start working on that little problem right now."

"If it is at all possible, Dr. Cameron, if you will let someone push me down the hall to look in on Macie."

"Ah, Mrs. Delang," he replied, "I prefer you remain immobile as to standing on those feet. Please, stay put and welcomes healing."

Charlotte had not experienced a blood clot before. She was swimming in despair. Now that Lily was gone and Macie was near, how could this happen. Surgery, the doctor explained brings strange reactions. You think you can trust your body? Well, it throws you a few curves. Your husband would understand that. Near and yet so far, she considered Macie. Just to see her sweet little face, to have her touch on the cheek, far better than shots in the stomach, pills to the mouth, more intravenous miracles in a bottle. Macie, hang on, for me…get well, we can do so many things together.

At one point she wanted to sleep. The doctor wanted her awake. She slid into the darkness watching Lily. "I've missed you," she whispered. "I miss you Momma." Lily climbed into bed beside her, her sweet breath on Charlotte's face. "You have to be strong, Momma. Macie needs you." It was real. Charlotte knew Lily wasn't there but she was. Charlotte must have spoken out loud, "You feel real. Your skin hasn't changed. Have you changed, Lily girl?"

"No, Momma. I'm still yours."

Evidently she needed the visit from Lily to start the healing. As Lily said, "Macie is waiting."

* * *

At the Granger home, Julie Wethington had brought her daughter and friends to visit with Elizabeth Granger. Elizabeth was enjoying the girls but Suz had not arrived. "Girls, mind your manners, Julie warned, "if you want to come back. I'll just see if there's laundry to do and check the kitchen for a light clean up." She had brought an apron and was tying it around her waist. All ready as she went down the stairs to the basement she heard conversation between the girls and Mrs. Granger.

"Do you think we are too old to play with dolls, Mrs. Granger?" Nash had actually put that behind her, all her dolls were on a shelf in the closet and she tried not to look at them when she opened the door."

"Why?" Elizabeth stared hard at Nash. "Why would you quit? What's so different playing with dolls than holding a real little baby? You're practicing for the day when you become a mother." It hit home, it was Nash's voice called her that evening and told her she had a little grand daughter, but not Lily."

"Just try very hard to stay with your child, Mrs. Granger. Mrs. Delang needs you. You must try very hard to encourage her, because she has not had enough time to mourn losing Lily." Nash shook the bottle of polish gently. "Just lay your hand on the table," she said. "You can still watch Audi and Bentley."

"Where do you get those words, Nash? The encouraging ones." Elizabeth peered into space, seeing nothing and in fact at this very moment trying to hang on. "I lose words and I lose people." Her expression appeared blank; no one could look into the distance and see what she was seeing. "I lost Lily. The man said I'm taking you home, Mrs. Granger. Why didn't he bring Lily, too?"

"Did you know the man?" Nash asked. "If you do, our secret club will find that person and watch that he does only good in the future." Na.sh gave Galanti a knowing glance. "Make a note," she whispered

"No, I don't know who he was. Why do you think he was there?" She tried to think."Times like these it's like a black fog rolls in, somethings there in my memory I almost pull up and then it goes." She peered hard at Nash. "Your name sounds like a car. Wasn't there one named Nash Rambler?"

"I'm only eleven and a half, Mrs. Granger. I don't know anything about that car except you're right I'm named after a car." She saw Mrs. Granger's surprise. "That's not my real name, but everyone calls us girls by the name of the car we chose."

"That's really strange. What is your real name?"

"I can't tell you, they'd kick me out of the club." Nash finished polishing Mrs. Granger's fingernails."Will Mrs. Delang be home soon?"

"You mean, like today?" Elizabeth tried to remember what she'd been told. "I think she has to stay at the hospital or maybe a motel…close to the doctor I think I was told. I don't remember a lot."

"Can you tell us anything to help in our hunt for whoever abducted Lily?"

"Just be careful. I don't know why the man didn't kill me and take Lily with him." Her attention span was shifting. "How old are you girls?" Lily was nine, ten in December. Tall for her age, but Charlotte is tall."

Nash was closing the lid on the nail polish tight. "You know, Nash," Elizabeth said. "In life there's not much we really know. What I know would fit in a thimble but Jacob, now there's a smart man."

"You like him?" Nash asked. "What if he is responsible for Lily on that bench?" Nash rose up. "You ask our age. Bentley and I are closest in age, come our birthdays we will be twelve and then just think…..teenagers. Audi and Suz are the youngest at age ten, and Galati is eleven. Lily was the youngest but we took her in because we liked her. There now, Mrs. Granger, your nails are done, your hair is coming along and your clothes are laid out. I'll wait with the others while you dress."

"That leaves Macie. She was a year older than Lily. I don't know her, Nash. What if she doesn't like me? I'll still be her grandmother, won't I?" She waved at Suz coming through the door.

"I like you." Nash called to the others. "Girls do you like Mrs. Granger?" A chorus of yes, followed.

"You know they tricked me," Elizabeth Granger continued speaking as though she hadn't just received a nice vote of popularity. "Charlotte didn't tell me she had Macie because Jacob took her away from her; my daughter, Charlotte, the baby's very own mother. I guess she was afraid I would go off in a deep end."

"What does that mean, Mrs. Granger?" Nash had drawn a small tablet from her pocket and was keeping notes of what Mrs. Granger spoke of. "I mean deep end is one thing but how are you using it?"

"I believe that is called colloquialism, Nash, did you know I was a teacher? When we use a phrase that sounds more like slang, for us to understand each other, that's colloquialism."

"You mean like a fish out of water?"

"Yes." The two laughed together. At that moment there was no age difference.

The hours passed rather quickly, Nash thought. There were times Mrs. Granger sat staring into space and one could only imagine what she was thinking.

"How many days until Charlotte comes home?" She asked the same question each hour. Nash was very patient and always replied. "Mrs. Granger you said you thought she must stay perhaps a week."

"I miss Charlotte," Mrs. Granger said, "But I miss Lily more. We played together." She gave a heavy sigh, closed her eyes and appeared after a time to be sleeping. Then she whispered, "It's a pity we don't always have sunshine. It was moonlight the night I left Lily lying there on that old bench. Why, her feet almost touched the ground. She was tired and just went to sleep. The man said she would be okay."

Didn't it bother you, Mrs. Granger, leaving Lily on that old bench?" Suz asked. "It still bothers me."

* * *

Charlotte passed each day waiting for Jacob to come for her. She was agreeable to the constant check the medical team kept on her. "Do you know how my daughter is doing?" She asked and the reply was always the same, "as well as can be expected, Mrs. Delang. Doctor Cameron is keeping an eye on her."

"I haven't seen her father the last days. Do you know if he is there with Macie, or did he have to go home to his parents?" Busy with their charts the medical team did not reply. Charlotte decided patience was her best effort, considering all they had been through.

The week ended. "You are ready for the trip home," Dr. Cameron said on one of his rare visits. "I am sending a couple prescriptions in case you need them.. Now, do you have someone to drive you home?"

"Yes, a friend is coming for me but first, Dr. Cameron, I wish to see my daughter. Can you give me directions?"

Dr. Cameron appeared not to have heard Charlotte's question. He was already out the door. The nurse lingered.

"Why would Dr. Cameron avoid my question?" Charlotte was deeply puzzled. "But he did, didn't he?"

The nurse gathered her things together and headed toward the door. She heard Mrs. Delang's voice, "Well, you know why, don't you? Someone with money has reentered the picture. They have promised him the moon and it very well may be he will come up missing as part of the process."

Charlotte's next words carried a threat. "I am one step away from making the call that will change lives and not necessarily in a good way. A few people may go to prison for participating." She waited. The Nurse turned toward her. "Go ahead. Speak. I know you have some information that I don't."

"I was curious, because I was present when your husband declared he would either take you to see the child or bring the child to you. As the days progressed and neither your husband nor the child appeared, I wondered where they were. Against principle I went there. I could not find either one."

""I really didn't know what to look for, a little girl who had a painful experience with surgery only a few days previous and a daddy that resembled that famous ball player, Jacob Long. I put my quest on Face Book and I worded it as a foolish fan, has anyone seen Jacob Long? The replys I received said, "no."

"I am quite truthfully wondering if I had a blood clot or a manufactured illness by Dr. Cameron."

The nurse took a quick breath, "Oh, no, Mrs. Delang, I sincerely doubt Dr. Cameron doing that."

"Why?" The old resentments surfaced for a moment, cynical of trusting anyone, hadn't she learned that, years previous when they all seemed to circle and turn against her cementing Jacob's case and allowing him to walk away with Macie. Did history repeat its self? "Think about it," she said, "He has a clinic to run, the financial end of the studies must be overwhelming. Why wouldn't he accept a tidy sum that would help in many ways?"

"No, Ma'am. Not Doctor Cameron." She had placed the supplies back on Charlotte's tray and was now wringing her hands together. "One thing I'll stake my reputation on as a nurse is his integrity."

"I've learned if the price is right, even integrity is purchased."

* * *

Bentley's mother came for Charlotte. "Do you need to go down the hall to see Macie before we leave?"

"No."

"No?" Elise seemed startled. "I don't mind pushing the wheel chair, Charlotte. I've had experience when Dad was ill."

"They're not there," Charlotte said. "No one will tell me why they have left when Macie was to stay several weeks." Her expression was stark, no gleam in the eye.

How do you describe despair, Elise was wondering. "Where are they?" She was speechless, no comfort or encouraging words came to mind, just where? Charlotte was quiet waiting for the nurse with the wheelchair to take her to the curb and then inside Elise's car she would know what to do.

Elise was backing around a car loading another patient into the front seat. "Any place you want to go?"

"Are you serious?" Charlotte asked. Elise nodded affirmative. "Would seventy miles be too far?"

"This is your day even if it is dark when we arrive home, let's just pray Jared and Bentley are already in bed. I designated this day to you, my friend. Complete. Do you understand?" She peered down on Charlotte. "Nod your head up and down. Good girl. Let's punch in the address and go seventy miles. Okay?"

They were comfortable with each other. They commented on something by the roadside now and then, and they rode in silence. "There it is, down the lane. See the blue trim? Mary's favorite color." She grinned as Elise studied the door. "Beautiful, huh? He has a real talent. Wood comes to life in his hands."

No one told her the blue color was fading. Possibly they hadn't noticed. Still, the home was beautiful. Elise walked slowly beside her. Charlotte knocked. "There's a key under a flat stone by the first step," she said. Elise hopped down the steps, retrieved the key and handed it to Charlotte.

"Welcome to Comfort Kitchen," Charlotte quipped. "It's so much more than that, but comfort food has always come out of that room and the blessing rests on the guest, whether family or friend."

"Sounds nice," Elise offered, as the door opened to more of Jacob's father's hand work. "I am impressed," she followed Charlotte through the rooms. "Why do you think no one's here?"

Charlotte opened the refrigerator. It was empty, not even a jar of pickles was on the shelf. She went on to the laundry room, spotless and last to Mary and Fraley's bedroom to open the doors to their closet and look up to the shelf near the ceiling where Mary kept their set of luggage, used but wiped clean until the next trip. The luggage was gone "That was the ultimate test? They have fled, but why?"

Her feet seemed to lag as she dragged her body down the hall to the guest room she had shared on occasion visits with Jacob after their marriage. The white crib was still there in one of the corners and the small white table Mary painted for Charlotte's convenience in bathing and changing diapers.

"They're gone." She whispered, the tears she'd been holding back, sliding down her cheeks now. "I can't believe he'd do this to me. How can I bear this disappointment, Elise? He didn't even let me see her." Elise pulled her down to sit on the side of the bed, the two of them with Elise's arm wrapped tight around her friend. Trying hard not to make a sound, tiny little moans of disappointment escaped her..

"I don't understand it, Hon," Elise managed. Her heart ached for Charlotte as all the injustice the woman had endured came forward to batter her soul. "There's a reason, Charlotte, don't let your mind go rogue before you have a chance to hear why they'd leave what they worked so hard to build. It doesn't make sense."

"What if I never find them? Macie won't have an opportunity to know I love her and always have."

"Never is a long time. I like to think forever is God's word and anything is possible. Don't you dare give up hope. You're a strong woman, my friend and I'm counting on you. It may take time but you will overcome this, too." They heard thunder roll. "It's not suppose to rain," Elise said.

"My goodness, it is building. What is that sound on the roof? My goodness it is torrential…a flood from heaven." Staring at Charlotte, she asked, "Are you afraid?" Wind was battering the sides of the house. "No, you are not. Not seeing Macie is worse than this, isn't it? Elise hurried back to Charlotte's side. "Should we be upstairs or is it safer down there?" She pointed to the stairs that led to the basement."I've never been in such a storm, Charlotte."

They heard a tree fall as lightening struck. "My whole life has been a storm," Charlotte whispered.

* * *

Outside, the wind was whipping the big trees around as the thunder seemed to center around them. "What is this?" Elise tried to see out the window, but now dark claimed any vision beyond the trees. "Is this a tornado?" She asked, turning to study Charlotte. Charlotte's face was stark white but the crying had stopped. They felt the house tremble as lightening hit, thunder rolled louder and rain lashed at the kitchen door sending a spew of small riverlets under the sill. "Is that normal?" Elise felt a rise of fear. "I think it's getting worse out there instead of better. What about this water?"

"There's a sump pump in the basement," Charlotte replied. "Maybe we should check it out." Carefully, she began the descent, down stairs with her friend by her side clutching her arm as if her life depended on it. "Oh, my goodness, look at that!" They stood on the last step staring at the barrel like fixture where the sump pump sit inside an enclosure.

Nothing was stirring, no water moving out, instead incoming water from the wall drains was churning into the barrel but there was no electrical cord plugged into the outlet to carry out the excess. "We have to get it hooked back up, or water will move through the floors, up the walls and take over left as it is." Charlotte was looking for the electrical outlet when she found a rectangular box, its clasp rusty and locked tight on the other side of the step from where they stood. "We need black tape, maybe something to scrape the wires, I don't know." She was trying to get the clasp open. "This is one of Fraley's old tool box.

Finally managing to loosen the clasp, she rummaged through the box. "A pair of pliers would be nice and knowledge to do this." She heaved a deep sigh. "This is something Fraley would never have left undone. I'd say in their hurry to depart he forgot all about it and when he remembers, he will be miserably upset. Mary and Fraley will want to return to their home."

"You knew your in-laws that well?"

"Once, I did. Both Fraley and Mary were real sticklers for getting a job done." Charlotte sank down on the step, examinining the cord. "All I can do is try to figure it out. What a mess."

"I'm watching this," Elise replied, "but I think you are talking about more than an electrical cord."

"Can't understand any of it," Charlotte whispered, focusing on the cord, "If you are thinking about this present situation of everyone gone. All I can do is ask why?"

"Something tells me there's a whole lot more to this, Charlotte. I don't understand how Jacob could do this but knowing his life these last year's I'd say there are extenuating circumstances attached. No way would elderly parents leave their home when you see they've put their life blood into it. Before you go after Jacob with a vengeance hire someone to find out who is really behind this."

* * *

The ride back to Perish was not without enlightment as to what the storm had wrought. There were tree limbs down, an occasional roof showing damage and the water roaring down side ditches headed toward the larger ones that carried to the river. Elise called home. No one answered. She called Jared at the Mayor's office. "How are things? Did it storm there?" She listened to her husband. When she closed her cell phone, she turned to Charlotte. "It seems the storm was wide spread. Power is off in Perish but he says it could be a lot worse. Mostly roads are closed and people trapped in town."

"Aren't you in charge of Emergency Services through the Ladies United?" Charlotte asked.

"Yes, but there's always a preliminary schedule as to how we handle the situation. Rose Mary Barnes will be contacting all the ladies willing to help. We do have a list of volunteers. Then the food will begin to come in and our age old plan to serve those in need will kick in. You are not to worry, we will be home in plenty time. Jared said when he gets home, he will put two cakes in the oven for me to finish, see how it works?" Elise smiled. "Teamwork. Right?"

"Good old Jared," Charlotte replied. "You remember those days when we were first married and we would all get together?" She sighed, "We had no idea what life would bring, did we?"

> Where there are prophecies they will fail and
> knowledge will vanish away but love never fails

Chapter 11

An hour later they pulled onto Main Street. Two Police cars blocked the lanes and Troy Sanders was walking toward them.

"What's going on, Troy? It's not every day I get stopped by a hallowed Chief of Police." Elise laughed as Troy peered in the window and saw Charlotte.

"The good Lord alone knows what's going on," he replied. "I'm afraid we don't have good news." He drew a deep breath. "I'm glad you are back, Charlotte. We've been anxiously awaiting your return. I even called the Clinic to ask if you had left and they stated the laws of privacy until I told them I was chief of police of your home town, then they told me you had left."

"What's the bad news, Troy?" Elise was trying to contain her concerns.

"The girls are missing. Not a one has come home this afternoon and Mrs. Granger is missing."

"They're together," Elise managed to say. "Oh, no, I can't go through Charlotte's ordeal. Bentley will be home when I get there."

"No, Elise, Jared's the one was checking on the girls and found out they were all gone."

"I talked to him about an hour ago. He didn't tell me."

"We just found out. It was his understanding they were at Mrs. Granger's. Nash's mother was with them, but she was checking clothes in the washer down in the basement and when she went back upstairs she noticed it was quiet." Troy shook his head. "About that time Jared called to see why Bentley wasn't home. He thought it was the weather but when…. Julie couldn't find them……"

"It's my fault." Charlotte felt the pain of losing Lily as though it just happened. "I should never have ask you to watch over Mother."

"No, Charlotte. We ask if we could help. This is something completely unexpected. If Mrs. Granger is with them no harm will come to them." Still she cast worried eyes on Charlotte. "But do you have any idea where we should look for them?"

"Yes, I know where we must go." She opened the door to get out. "Troy, it will take a vehicle capable of driving in very adverse road conditions."

"What do you have in mind, Charlotte?" Troy was probably the only person had any idea what Jacob and Charlotte had suffered the night they found Mrs. Granger in the woods and had he not been a friend of Jacob's he doubt he would know. It was difficult; Jacob told him, let's not spread the word. Now, Charlotte was willing to sacrifice whatever they wished to keep secret, to find the girls. "Will it take more than a four wheel drive, Charlotte?" She nodded.

"I'm not even sure my idea would work but Troy, I remember years ago the city purchased an old army tank. It sit in front of the Police Station for five years according to mother. She and Dad were on one of the community advancement committees and she said eventually that piece of equipment was stored because it wasn't used and it had become a laughing stock in the community. But it was purchased for times such as these. Jacob just wasn't aware of it, when we were searching for mother the last time, and I forgot."

Troy was scratching his head. "That old tank, Charlotte? Who knows whether it would even run after all this time." He saw how intent she was. "Are the roads that severe, Charlotte?" She nodded. "Then we will look into it, after all it was designed for the Army, surely it is salvageable." He glanced at his watch. "Give us an hour, fuel will have to be emptied out, the tank cleaned and refueled. Whether we can find a suitable battery…"his words died off with a new thought. "Charlotte, you've just had surgery, you can't be riding through rough terrain…and if the weather kicks back in and there's rain. No, this is out of your hands."

"Do you know the way?" He stood there staring at her. Finally he shook his head.

"I don't," he said. "Can you draw us a map?"

"I'll do better than that, I'll show you. If Jacob hadn't explained the route to me the next day, I wouldn't know. We weren't on the best of terms, but in case it ever happened again, I needed information."

* * *

Charlotte changed into jeans and a heavy sweatshirt. Temperatures were cooler in the forest. Pulling on an old pair of leather boots she was ready. She found Troy and Jared with a group of towns people, among them every parent of the five girls. They stared at her. Troy saw her fear and came to meet her. "It's all right, Charlotte. They're just scared. Before Lily, nothing like this happened in Perish."

"I'm scared, too and embarrassed. It's my mother who is the adult and no doubt in charge of the idea."

"You feel really sure they will have gone back to where your mother was last time?"

"Yes, that is one thing I don't doubt. She loved that place. She would want to show it off."

"Here's the plan," Troy said. "You and I will go first in the tank, hopefully it will clear the way for those who follow. I'm thinking fill in the deep ruts Jacob mentioned and continue on. How does that sound?"

"It sounds like a bad dream but I know it isn't," she replied. "Can you hold my hand while I climb?"

* * *

They cleared town, passed by Charlotte's parent's home and entered the woods.

"Is this family land, Charlotte?" She nodded. "I didn't know there was anything back her except trees but Jacob said it was your mother's get away built by your daddy and a pretty nice place at that."

"I didn't know about it, Troy, until the night we were searching for Mother, but Jacob knew. He said Dad built it while I was with Jack and they never mentioned it but it cost a pretty penny to build."

Troy was watching the sky; lightening was beginning in the West. "If we can just get them loaded up and out before the next storm comes in. What do you plan to do with your mother, Charlotte? Do you think she has reached a point she's dangerous to herself?"

"She will die if we put her in a place she has no freedom. To me, she hasn't reached that point."

"Man oh man," Troy realized the road conditions had blurred into one huge problem of deep ruts that spread the width of the age old path and downed trees from the day's storm."Some of these we can go over but if we run into one of those giant oaks it is certainly going to take awhile to clear and every minute counts due to getting dark soon." He glanced to Charlotte; she was trying to hold her stomach area from movement. "Sorry," he said, his eyes troubled. "I really feared your coming along."

"Troy, I feel responsible. I thought mother was much better. But I judged wrong and now the girls are in danger. I had to come along." The fact they could barely hear each other's words didn't help. "I have to see that they are all well and no unexpected mishaps."

"Do you think we are close, Charlotte? I studied your map, but parts of it made no sense to me."

"It's an eighty acre tract of wooded land, Troy; the government won't let us destroy for planting acreage." She pointed ahead. "The problem, according to Jacob, Dad not having proper equipment he laid out the road according to natural openings and that's why it became a maze of sorts."

"Understandable," Troy replied.

The ride for Charlotte brought memories of the night Lily was found. She would not allow herself to think the girls and her mother would suffer the same fate. Still she could not fathom her mother orchestrating a trip to the house in the woods, although it was her favorite place. There she dreamed out loud, there she had the freedom to do and say as she pleased without someone labeling her dementia. Charlotte could hear her mother explaining, "it is as if your daddy is still there."

Could this situation be connected to Jacob leaving the area with Macie. She knew Raymond Long's attempt to gain custody of Jacob attacked his very manhood that another person be in control of his life? She had seen the pain in his eyes, the thought of someone else telling him what to do when he was the one financially secure if the courts would turn loose of those higher up who had already gained control of those finances, in order to protect me, he had once said in despair when his head was throbbing and the pain medication was useless. It is not right. She saw the ugliness of what one person could do to another; looking on his pain forgetting her own and that he was the one to blame.

Then, as if watching a movie reel, she saw him at the kitchen table reach for her hand and say grace over their food and thank the Lord for life and its blessings. And last she heard his voice saying, "I've changed, Charlotte. I'm not that man anymore. I've been brought to my knees and now I know who I am."

* * *

Who was she? She could not analyze herself. She had done what she thought right for their daughter but few would understand her pain realizing Macie was gone; her reward was not to see her child. Now, as they found their way through the trees, Troy trying to flatten the deep ruts for those behind, Charlotte remembered Jacob's voice comforting her, whispering times past in her ear. He had not forgotten. Why? He had experienced much since their time together. She had listened as he whispered; I thought I would die without you in my life, Charlotte. Secretly she carried those words with her until she saw the empty rooms and her heart had whispered you thought perhaps he had cared but this proves he doesn't and he never did. Bind up your wounds and lock the door that he can never slip through again. And still, she reasoned and questioned, what if someone threatened Macie's security? Then, she knew Jacob would do what he must to protect their child. With all that in mind, she searched the landscape for familiar markings and ahead she saw the bend of trees.

"We are near the clearing and I don't mean to suggest anything clandestine, but if they aren't afraid and have had a good evening, Troy, could we check things out before we go inside, you know, be sure they are all right but not leave a lasting memory in their minds they'll have nightmares over the rest of their lives when we can handle this gently." Her eyes were pleading, "Not just for Mother, Troy, but for little girls to remember kindly as they grow up and tell the story."

"I understand, Charlotte. Jared's in the truck behind us and then the second would be my deputy. Perhaps Jared could go to the window and peer in, since he's not in uniform. Would that work?"

She nodded. "Thank you, Troy." She was relieved the clearing was, as she thought, around that last bend of trees. She could see candle glow in the windows, but something didn't make sense. There were fresh ruts coming from the North to the clearing as if someone had made a new road from that direction.

Troy climbed out. "It's still a good ways, Charlotte. Are you sure you can walk that distance in the mud?" She nodded as he gave her a hand to climb down from the tank. "I'll tell the men our plan," he said, leaving her. She watched as Jared nodded and then headed toward the house. She was curious, watching Jared as he went from the first window to the second as if there might be a problem and then to a third, and whereas he had approached full height, he was now bending to the waist and hurrying back. It was then Elise stepped by her side and gripped her hand.

Almost a sob of relief came from Charlotte. "I should have known you would come along and I'm glad."

"There're two men in there," Jared said in a low voice. "I saw Mrs. Granger sitting in front of the girls as though they are playing school." He stared hard at Charlotte, "That's all I can think they are doing. Each girl has a paper and pencil but they don't seem afraid, nor does Mrs. Granger but I don't know the men as I could only see their backs. They were not facing me." He was shocked over the two. "How do we handle this, Troy?"

"Keep everyone quiet, Jared. Russell and I will go around the house to see if there's a vehicle or means of transportation. Jacob said teenagers use this land to increase their skill on four wheelers and even dirt bikes. According to him some of them compete and this is their best training ground."

Within minutes, Russel came trotting back. "Troy's taken the keys out of two vehicles parked on the North side of the house. He says we will split up, two go in the back door and two through the front. He doesn't thing they are armed but he feels their intentions are not good and he's wondering if they used some kind of ploy to bring Mrs. Granger and the girls out here. Charlotte, he wants you and Elise to wait until we get inside." He glanced to Jared and Suz's father. "Y'all ready?"

* * *

They waited as Troy asked. Two cleared front and two cleared the back entrance of the house. When signaled, Charlotte entered to find her mother and the girls playing school, as Jared said. They glanced up, only a moment's surprise to see Charlotte and Elise. Bentley ran to hug her mother and returned to where the girls were still involved in their game. Elise and Charlotte's eyes met.

"Something seems a bit off-key here, doesn't it?" Elise asked and Charlotte nodded. "Threatened, perhaps?" She whispered, "We will get to the bottom of this later. They are too calm."

"Just as I hoped," Elizabeth smile welcomed them. "They love this place as I do."

"But Mother, how did you get here and who are those men?"

"What men?" Mrs. Granger glanced around the room. "We rode in that man's truck, the one that called. He said, "Daddy's waiting for you Elizabeth. Tell the girls we have a nice surprise for them and remember be very quiet. We aren't taking Julie with us." Elizabeth Granger seemed regretful for a moment. "Is that why you are here, because we left her behind and hurt her feelings?"

For a moment it all seemed surreal. Charlotte glanced around. There were no men and yet they had arrived here. Then she heard the scuffle from the back. Troy and his deputy came into the room each with a reluctant and defying person in cuffs; Raymond Long and another man she could not place though she felt she had seen him before.

"It's all beginning to make sense, Charlotte. Why would Raymond Long have any interest in your mother and our town's girls? He wants something." Troy shook his head as if the whole thing was beyond him but this was his job and what he faced every day as a public servant. "Jared's going to press charges. Kidnapping."

Raymond Long's face went white. "It's not that way, Troy. We just took Mrs. Granger and the girls on a ride to her favorite place." He sneered, "You can't prove otherwise with a woman that's losing her mind." He began to laugh. "Kidnapping? You wish, Troy Sanders, I'll have your job, too."

Charlotte had heard enough. She slapped Raymond Long. His head snapped in surprise and his expression was priceless. "That's my mother you are talking about and I question your mentality in taking a woman who suffers lapse of memory, but most of all to take precious little girls that mean everything to their parents. What kind of man are you? I think your greed has finally caught up with you."

She turned to her mother. "Mother, do you remember what this man spoke with you about?"

"Why, he wants to buy this property, Charlotte and I told him it's not for sale. Why would he want it, anyway?" She stared out into the growing dark. "He doesn't make sense and that night he came for Lily he said let's just take a ride, Mrs. Granger, you don't get out much anymore and I'm here to help you out." Her eyes locked on Raymond Long. "He talks a lot about Jacob, Charlotte. He says the man is not fit to live and how he probably won't live much longer. I like Jacob. I told him." Elizabeth Granger had spent her last ounce of energy. "We just want to go home, don't we, girls?" The girls flocked to her side, their arms around her.

"I believe Jared that your charge against Raymond will hold. When the people hear what he's done, there will be many come forward to voice the injustice he has done toward them." He studied Raymond Long. "Your Daddy and I had a discussion about this once, Raymond, you can't keep mistreating people, one day it will catch up with you."

Elizabeth stood, "Time to go home, girls but we had a good time and we'll come again if you want to."

"They are so docile," Elise remarked. "I mean, they don't seem concerned over anything and that's not like these girls." She glanced to Charlotte, "you know their secret club and all that…"

"It's the drinks." Elizabeth said. "He insisted we all drink the juice he brought. Doctor's orders he said, let's play doctor and I'll be the doctor and just like that he told us all we had to drink the juice to prevent getting sick. It was the same that night with Lily. He insisted we all drink the juice."

Charlotte's gasp was heard by all. "That's it. The coroner said there are no broken bones but there's only one way to find out if it was some kind of drug or internal problem that killed Lily. I couldn't bear to see anything more done to my Lily."

"Hard as it sounds, Charlotte, a confession is as good as an autopsy in this case."

"Who confessed?" Raymond asked. His cold demeanor had resurfaced, "an old lady that can't remember her name half the time tells you that? It won't hold water."

"We'll see," Jared stepped closer to Raymond. "If the law wasn't here to stop me, I'd beat you to a pulp. A far as I'm concerned, you kidnapped my daughter. I don't know what the other parents will say."

"Your threats are so far out there. Who are you?" Raymond tried to stare him down. "Do you realize how ridiculous this all sounds, highly respected mortician in small town America plots evil toward his fellow citizens?" Raymond Long snorted. "Just think to yourself, who you are compared to me and who do you know? I have a long line of politicians behind me."

"Get him out of here. Elise are you up to driving your truck back and let Jared bring Raymond's? We will have to leave the other fellows." Troy's patience with Raymond Long had reached an impasse.

"He don't deserve a truck like that anyway." Russel muttered. "Came into town broke and now that…"

"Now Russel, it's not our place to judge how the man got his wheels but we need a thorough search…"

"Troy," Charlotte interrupted. "We need to take his vehicle too; otherwise someone might say evidence was tampered with, if there proves to be any evidence."

"We are short a driver, Charlotte."

"No, I can drive something." For the first time Charlotte saw a bit of humor, "But not the tank."

"Girl," Elise hugged her friend tight. "You have got to get some rest, that old school girl silliness is claiming you and I'll have to admit, me too. I think we've had a bigger slice of life than we need tonight."

Troy saw the girls to the truck Jared would be driving. Bentley rode with her mother and Mrs. Granger to his surprise said, "I'll ride with you Troy. I've always heard about these tanks. I want to experience firsthand what I've been told." Troy glanced Charlottes way and found her hiding a grin. He shook his head and gave Elizabeth Granger a hand up.

"We will be quite the little convoy arriving back in town." Troy said. "Russel do you have your suspects properly handcuffed and that means firm, that they don't consider knocking you in the head and escaping.

"You bet, Sir." Russel gave the two in the back seat an appraisal. "It's time they get what they deserve."

Troy couldn't agree more but it was his sacred duty to uphold the law and see each man was fairly served. "We will let the Judge decide that," he said but secretly he remembered Langston and Raymond had always been at odds and he knew that judicial fairness would be tempted, but Langston would do what was right. A few good men, he thought and his soul was satisfied. He was one of them.

He heard Raymond telling Russel he was allowed a call.

"No service in these woods," Russel replied. Good answer, Troy thought, and then he heard Russel's peal of laughter and all he could do was shake his head. Russell was enjoying Raymond Long's discomfort.

"Ready, Mrs. Granger?"

She gave him a bright smile. "I'm ready, Troy. Let's see what this old tank can do."

Troy was almost relieved they could not hear each other above the engines. His mind was in turmoil.

What kind of drink would make people lethargic? That's what he had seen. The girls were quiet, almost in a stupor. At first he had thought of hypnosis but they were able to function, though slow. He knew in the back of his mind something was stirring that he encountered a couple years back when a girl in town was rushed to the hospital. She had been on a date when the drinks were served. Her parents considered it alcoholic poisoning saying she was not one to drink but the doctor had mentioned something else. It had been another one of those crazy calls where the parents chose to cover it up.

It was on the tip of his tongue but he couldn't pull it out. Almost seemed like a woman's name. Now why would that be? By the time they pulled into Perish, he was mentally exhausted along with the physical. First there were the parents and their child reunited, a heartwarming time he appreciated because he knew it could have been worse. He asked if they could wait around a few minutes in case they were needed and would they follow Jared over to the City Hall. Then there was the booking of Raymond Long and his accomplice. "Who is the second guy?" He asked Russel."

Russel grinned. "That fellow I warned you about."

"If it's who you tried to get me to arrest without just cause, well, now you can be happy," Troy replied. "So what's his name?"

"Dawsey Dwain Koonce, the second, what works for old Oscar and Raymond Long. Meet your new mortician, Chief."

Troy stood there making the connection in his head. That's where it was. Russell had passed on information, "that stringy fellow what we see around the Long's, he's known over in Rayville for selling that drug what makes people comply…"

"What in the world are you really saying?" Troy had demanded. "You and your mystery words."

"Why, I just hated to tell our Chief of Police about the drug labeled for date rape, you know, it makes them sexually active, except most aren't complyin, maybe even some are dyin.'

"Tell me you haven't personally experienced this drug you're mentioning?"

"No sir, no roofies for me. I know people die from them." That conversation was weeks ago.

Now he asked, "Is your cell working?" Russel nodded. "That Nurse, that lives down the way, works for Doc Heller. Call her; ask her if we need a blood sample from these girls, tonight? And if we do, does she need the doctor to come do it or can she? Whatever is legal. But it's got to stand up in court. I'll get back over there and detain the parents and their daughters. This is an emergency, Russel. It is the thing to do."

Troy's heart thundered, he felt it gain pace and race beneath the soiled uniforms pocket. Was it possible, Raymond Long had access to a drug that might kill whoever he administered it to? Breathe, he told himself. Breathe deep. No need you having a heart attack over Raymond Long. But it wasn't Raymond. It was what happened to Lily. It made sense and it could have happened to those five little girls with their funny little names and the club they had formed to find out who hurt Lily. Who killed Lily, he corrected, if what Russel was saying was true. For a second he felt the need to lean on something.

"You all right, Chief?" Russel being over six feet tall was peering down into his face. "You look a little peaked, like maybe your plannin' to fall over."

"I'm trying to piece it all together. Mrs. Granger identified Raymond as the one who drove her and Lily around that night but we can't even think what a prosecuting attorney would do with Mrs. Granger on the stand.

Dementia or first stage of Alzheimer's." Troy sit down and put his head in his hands. "What a night."

"Yes sir, but Mrs. Granger didn't seem crazy to me. She may rally after awhile and be just fine. I had an aunt what lost her child in a drowning," Russel paused, remembering, taking off his cap and holding it while he finished speaking. "After a good long while, she came back to herself, but that first year she was not herself, no sir. She wandered away just to be alone and think of little Alice. She was my Momma's sister and she said, weren't nothing wrong with Ellie, just give her time and sure enough."

Troy was silent, thinking. Nash had him run plates on a resident. The name was Mrs. Dawsey Koonce. Did she have another name? Why had Nash and the club singled out this woman? Tomorrow, he would bring the girls in to discuss their investigation.

Tonight, it was his duty to see Mrs. Granger and Charlotte home. Tomorrow he would question the Koonce fellow and if there was anything there, then they would, Lord help him, he felt weak in the knees thinking what could have happened to those little girls. He had two of his own. God protect them.

On his way out, he said, "Russel, find the medical name for that date rape drug, print me out a sheet. Don't let a cell phone fall into Raymond's hands; with our power out he can't call on a land phone. I want him to sit overnight in that cell. You got that?"

Russel nodded. Troy shook his head. Russel might come across as a Barney Fife but he had a degree in business, was a computer whiz and if the entire world found wrong with him was that he had a weird compulsion to use his verbs wrong, then they needed to look beneath Russel's exterior. He was a genius.

He found Elise and Jared waiting. "Is there more?" He asked. They pointed to Charlotte and her mother.

"Charlotte saw her mother was worn thin, she meant to help her get comfortable; in the process they both fell asleep. I think Charlotte's pre-surgery dismissal from the hospital could have intended she go straight home and rest. Anyway, that's what the paper she gave to me says. Instead we've had a tromp through the woods. We are taking them home. They need supervision to get to bed tonight."

"You need to stay a few minutes longer, Elise. There's a nurse coming to take blood samples."

"That means you've found something, Troy." Jared stepped closer. "Can you tell us?"

"Doc Heller's nurse?" He looked to Elise to identify her. "She's the one will be here." A car pulled into the drive. "That's her. I don't know her name."

"Jean Atwell, a cousin to the Prosecuting Attorney but she's pretty rigid and she is an RN."

Troy wondered for a minute if he had made a mistake but there was little else he could have done this time of night. "I may have to run those samples over to Greenway, myself, tonight for security reasons." He took a deep breath and started toward Miss Atwell. "Thank you for coming on short notice. My deputy explained we've had a bit of an upset here?" She appeared to be looking for the girls.

"We ask the parents to walk their girls over to City Hall. You know Jared Stiles, our mayor?"

Miss Atwell nodded. "What's wrong with the Police Station?" She asked, "We're all ready here."

"No, Ma'm, we can't take the children in there, tonight. It's the City Hall just a walk away." Behind her back, Jared nodded and headed toward his building. Troy took another deep breath.

"I'll get my car and supplies." She hurried to her car and drove the half block to where Jared was opening the door for her. Elise and Troy arrived by the time she was set up. She didn't call for anyone to come forward, she stared at the parents. Jared realizing the other little girls were tired and reluctant to go forward took Bentley by the hand and walked with her to the nurse's station.

"She's the niece of Raymond Long's friend the Prosecuting Attorney, right?" Troy muttered, his voice low and then blew out a breath of hot air. "The good Lord help me, I sure know how to pick 'em."

Jared came out holding a tearful Bentley's hand. Troy couldn't stand it. "Jared, I'll take it from here. When the others leave, I'll turn the alarm system on and lock up. You all have been a great help. Thanks for standing by me."

"Pull rank, if you have to, Troy. Chief of Police, in this situation is over a Nurse drawing blood samples."

"I'll remember you said that," Troy agreed.

Elise yawned, "If it's all the same with you, Troy, Jared and I plan to spend the night out there when we take them home. Bentley's asleep in the front of the truck and she'll be in our bed tonight, even if it is at Mrs. Grangers." She yawned again. "It's a king size in the guest room and that will work just fine, wont' it, hon?" She realized Jared was quiet and had been since he learned Raymond had drugged the children. "I'll drive," she said. "We are leaving my car here, Troy."

"Thank you," he said. "I was going to go with them but I couldn't spend the night. That's mighty fine of you both."

"I told them to get in the back seat of the truck. They didn't even complain. Some things just work out, don't they?" She and Jared loaded in, Jared taking a sleeping Bentley onto his lap. "Goodnight, Troy."

Troy watched them drive away. Greater love hath no man than he lay down his life for a friend. Where did that come from? Tired, though he had been freed from one task, he headed back inside. Russel heard the door open and came to meet him, thrusting a sheaf of papers in his hand.

Knowledge will vanish for we know in
part and we prophesy in part

Chapter 12

"Ro-hip-nol," he said. "It's spelled R-o-h-y-p-n-ol with the word flunitazepam in parenthesis. You will be sick after readin about it. Long story short, it is hard to detect because it has no taste or smell. It can cause weakness and unconsciousness, givin in excess it could kill a person. I was thinkin a small child like Lily."

Troy held up a hand. "I'm sick already. Soul sick to think we have men who are monsters in our midst."

* * *

It was seven o'clock. Elise opened the dryer. Shaking the clothes she wondered if Jared would notice the wrinkle around the collar of his shirt. Otherwise the clothes looked good. They'd all three had a shower before piling into the King sized bed. She and Bentley had raided underwear from Charlotte and Lily's rooms and she had found what Jared needed from Jack's last remaining stash of clothes. She had feared they might not sleep but the trauma of the night had worn them thin. The drive through the woods had been a physical endeavor. Mentally exhausted, they would never forget last night. They slept.

She knew by now Troy would be well into last night's case. He would need to speak with the girls and she would be there to buffer the way along with any other parent. Troy was a good man but he too could use a friend, one who kept their mouth shut and stood by, she and Jared knew that fact, too well.

Going back upstairs she found Jared in the kitchen, smiling they embraced and kissed. It was their morning ritual except in someone else's home. "Bentley's still asleep," he whispered, nuzzling her neck. "What do we need to do?"

"I've borrowed two mixes from Mrs. Granger's pantry and the cakes are ready to cool and then frost." She turned toward the oven and cleared the timer ready to go off. "There's coffee to your left, and cereal. I've cleaned away the mixing bowls and utensils, so we will eat cereal or pick up something in town. The cakes are in disposable pans. I can replace everything, for Mrs. Granger, but in order to help Troy with the girls I thought I should have this task behind me."

Jared hugged her again before going to pour the two cups of coffee. "We didn't have to talk last night about the seriousness of Raymond Long's drugging our girls, but I think Troy was worried once he saw it was the Prosecuting Attorney's cousin came to draw the blood. Did you have that impression?"

"I did," she replied. "But what could he do? He said if possible, he would deliver the samples himself."

"Raymond's influence will be felt. As parents we need to all stick together but a lot of that will depend on who owes money to the Long's and many have funeral insurance with him they could lose if he hasn't used the money properly and should he go away and can't cover for it."

"What do you mean?" She slid into the chair opposite Jared. "Nothing compares to their child's life."

"Alive or available to the people, the Long's can cover for money collected if one of the people they have collected from dies, but if the Long's kept the money and used it themselves and Raymond goes to prison there's no one here to see their money paid in is honored."

"Why would they do that? I thought the money they collect went to an insuring company just as any other insurance."

"It's supposed to, but there have been rumors for years why the Long's refuse to do a yearly statement as to the individual's balance."

"So what you are saying is, the community people who use that service believe when they die they've paid for their funeral already, but what they may have been doing in truth was funding the Long family."

"Exactly." He glanced at the arm of clothes she had brought up. "My love, you have been busy."

She grinned. "Old habits die hard, but its time to wake Bentley and get on the road. Charlotte will take it from here with her own needs and her mothers. I'll check with her later. Let's go strip the bed again and we can head in to City Hall within the next thirty minutes. Before we leave I'll start the washer for those bedclothes and the ones we borrowed."

"Sounds like a plan." Rising he reached for her hand. "Have I told you lately how much I love and appreciate you?"

"Tell me again," she whispered coming into his arms. "I'm a real bonehead for all this mushy stuff."

* * *

Russel was hesitant to leave. Troy had been up all night too. He had taken the blood samples of the girls to Greenville. They would know the results by noon. The power was back on and Raymond Long was involved in his phone call. He stood with his back to the room, but it was apparent the call wasn't going as expected. "What do you mean? Let me tell you, I haven't donated to your campaigns for nothing." He slammed the phone on its cradle.

"Looks like trouble in Central City," Russel quipped. "I'm stayin, Chief. I couldn't sleep if I went home."

Troy glanced down, he'd missed a button on the shirt but the hot shower had been a God send. He believed he could make it a few more hours. Raymond stood in front of his desk. "I need to make a call to the Sheriff. It seems you didn't follow correct procedure bringing us in here."

"No?" Troy raised his eyes to Raymond. "How's that, we should have left you there in the woods? Now that would have been harsh, Raymond, leaving you handcuffed to the closet rod and driving your vehicle back for you."

"You will live to regret this day, Sanders."

"From the sound of that phone call you were blaring out, I'm wondering if perhaps you might regret a few things too, Raymond." Troy studied the man in front of his desk. "What sane man picks up five little girls and takes them on a ride without their parent's permission?"

"There's not a soul will go against me, you'll see."

The morning stretched into its usual humidity. They hadn't heard much from the Koonce fellow. Troy decided while he was waiting for the girls he'd question Koonce. Visibly shaking, Troy asked Russel, "does our other prisoner seem shaken to you?"

Russel laughed, "He's coming down. It's time for a fix and we're fresh out."

Troy groaned, "Don't say things like that where people can hear you. We don't store drugs." He shook his head, "you need to go home get some sleep, anyway rest. Send in that Koonce fellow. We're going to have a little talk."

There was a faint knock at the door. Nash stood there peering through the glassed window. "Mr. Troy, could I speak with you a minute?" Troy went to the outer room. "Mr. Troy, there's something our club has uncovered I think you need to know. Some of the girls can't come later for our appointment."

"Let's sit over there at that table, Nash and you tell me whatever it is and I'll be happy to listen.'" Troy shook her hand. "You and the girls have done good work. Continue to be safe and we will talk again."

* * *

Charlotte awakened to the sound of the washer's whirl, slowing down and then the usual abrupt stop. She could barely remember Elise guiding her toward the shower saying, "Remember to take off your clothes before you step into the water." Elise had laughed, "but if you forget, remember to take the wet ones off before you fall into bed." She was thankful for a friend that stood by you.

Apparently they had already left and Elise had stripped the bed clothes and set the washer to run. "The revolving bed," she said aloud. Jacob had slept there. Bone tired as she was last night, she did remember wondering if Raymond Long had anything to do with where Jacob and Macie were. Now, she stretched, dreading having to get up but she must check on Mother.

Her feet on the floor was one thing, but standing she wanted to bend double, the stiffness that claimed her body was enough that she sank back down on the bed. She heard no sound down the hall to her mother's room. Dare she lay back and let her body decide what to do next? One hand where the incision was, the other letting her down onto the mattress gently, she sank against the pillow, her mind and body were weary. The doctor's orders for rest into the next week seemed a good thing at the moment as her eyes closed and a dream formed to chase across her mind; It was as though she reviewed the past, caught somewhere viewing a life she really had not known and yet the understanding was part of who she was; Macie dancing with her daddy, smiling and happy, Lily joining in. She had never told him and she wouldn't. Jack was a good man and he deserved her loyalty. She loved Jack but their love was different, more settled; unlike the love she'd known for Jacob in those first years, passionate, exciting sometimes they had laughed over the smallest thing coming together to hold each other, look into each other's eyes and declare their undying love. Then, Jacob's future looked brighter, he had left her behind, or had she chosen to stay behind. "Partying is for the wild group," she said, primly. "I can't drag Macie from bar to bar."

"It's not like that," he'd denied. "Nice restaurants, yes, an occasional dinner party in an influential home, yes."

"I don't have to influence anyone." She said, listening as he said, "but I do."

The years had passed, her with Jack and Lily but somewhere out there she had another child, Macie. The dreams faded into darkness, she slept, restless, her hand clutching her stomach for that lost part of her self. "Charlotte. Charlotte. Wake up. I need to talk to you." Someone was holding her.

Friday begins.

Elizabeth Granger viewed a sleeping Charlotte. Drawn into a fetal position, her daughter seemed to be sleeping peacefully and yet she thought it was Charlotte calling down the hall that awakened her.

She sank onto the side of the bed. "Charlotte, did you put me to bed last night?" Charlotte didn't stir.

Elizabeth arose to wander the hall toward the kitchen. And there, big as life sit Jacob Long. She tightened the belt to her robe and went in to see him as if it were an everyday occurrence. "Good morning, Jacob."

"Good morning, Elizabeth."

She smiled. "Am I dreaming, Jacob or, are you real?"

"I'm real," he said. "I tried to waken Charlotte, but I understand she had quite a busy day yesterday."

"How would you know?" She sat opposite Jacob at the table as he poured coffee into a cup and handed it to her. "How did you get here?"

"I've not been far away, Elizabeth."

"But I heard Charlotte and Elise and they said you were gone." She searched his face for honesty. "They went to your parent's home and they were also gone."

A reflective expression crossed Jacob's face. "There was danger to them, Elizabeth. It was best they leave quickly and no one know where they went."

"Why, Jacob?"

"I don't have all the answers, Elizabeth, but I came here to reassure Charlotte that Macie is all right and if it had not been necessary I would not have removed her from the surgery unit at Dr. Cameron's facility." He stood. "I hoped Charlotte would waken and I could tell her but it seems she had a full day yesterday and today her body needs rest." His eyes were sad as he wondered how much he could tell Elizabeth. "Please," he finally said, "tell Charlotte I tried but she wouldn't waken and all I'm asking is that she trust me. I have someone working on this and our greatest need right now is that we trust each other and wait for all the answers to the questions we've had. But I have to leave before there's someone here to find me." He stooped to place a kiss on Elizabeth's forehead. "Be safe, Elizabeth."

* * *

Troy Sanders questioned Dawsey Koonce the third. "That's an impressive name you have there, Koonce," he said. "Tell me a little about yourself. How and when did you meet Raymond Long?"

"When I applied for work, I was broke and the waitress down at that place where they sell gas and have carry out food said there's a man just ask about someone to work and pointed to Mr. Long and I went over and talked to him." He saw the Chief of Police of Perish waited for more information. "He said he needed someone to do a job for him and I told him I was the man." Koonce gave Troy a searching look. "Do I need a lawyer before I talk to you? I don't have money for one but if that's my right then you have to get one for me, don't you?"

"Have you committed some kind of crime to need a lawyer, Dawsey? Because we are just talking. I need to know how you came into Raymond's employment. Wasn't that what you wanted to explain to me?" Troy sat down opposite Dawsey. "Did you tell me what the job was?"

"He needed something."

"What was that he needed?"

Dawsey squirmed, uncomfortably. "I believe I shouldn't say as it was personal and him being my boss."

"Well, it will all come out in the Court room trial, anyway." Troy said. "Let's just talk about your truck. How's that?" Troy shook his head, "That is one nice set of wheels. You said you were broke, no money, but now you have a fine truck. Tell me the magic behind that because I could sure use one like it."

"I never thought I'd have a truck like that this soon. I...well, our family's poor. No one has anything."

"I differ with your way of thinking, there, Dawsey. You have life and a opportunity to do about what you want but you do usually have to start low and work your way forward." That means up."

Russel was in the room adjacent and could hear their conversation. Because Troy wasn't readin him his rights like Russel would have; to Russel, Troy sounded like Andy Griffith, no hurry, just visitin. No, sir, he would have shot the problem home by now but Troy said he'd do the questionin.

"Now, Dawsey, I was just wonderin' about that truck. Say, does your Momma have a vehicle?'

"Yes, she does some old thing that runs now and then but she wouldn't let me borrow it. She said I was too reckless and I was a good for nothin' that never would amount to nothin."

"So you never borrowed her car?"

"No, I didn't."

"Well, Dawsey, it seems I need to tell you, some of our investigators found your momma's car and in a front fender of that car they found a piece of Lily's dress and I can tell you who ever was driving that car is in a heap of trouble It seems that old car has been through a lot but one thing for certain, it took your mother places she needed to go affirmed by her long time friend but it seems your boss was driving the car that night. Would you like to change your mind and could you tell me what I need to know?"

Dawsey blanched a few shades whiter and hung his head miserably low to his chest before finally looking up into Troy's face. "My Momma ain't done nothing wrong; it's not her way, but Raymond Long kind of set her up and kept her old car one night and I think that's the night little Lily Delang died."

"Now Dawsey, how would a young fellow like you remember specifically?"

"It was him needin roofies and me havin to go over to the next town to get them for him. He said, Listen here boy, I got you a good truck so don't even act like you'd complain, just get your butt in that vehicle, high tail it over there and back, Pronto."Dawseys shoulders shook as he gasp for breath. "You think I need to warn my momma what's coming down the road?"

"It's not good, but I doubt Raymond will be bothering her."

"What's he going to do to me?"

"It seems you have reason for concern." Troy stared out the window thinking, then he studied the picture of the president hanging over the counter and finally his eyes returned to Dawsey. Dawsey had become a fidgeting mess, it was almost as if the young man was coming unglued.

"I can testify on stand," Dawsey said, "Raymond Long took my mother's car home that night, on the night little Lily Delang died. The same night I brought back the roofies earlier when he demanded I go for in another town and it is my belief he some way got little Lily to partake of them..." he stopped talking, his words had become a shaken mess. "That won't work, will it?" His eyes lifted to the Chief of Police Troy Sanders, "Because I don't know if he used my Momma's car to go out to the Delangs and pick up the grandma and her granddaughter, or not."

"Let's start at the beginning, you tell me your story, from the first time you spoke with Mr. Raymond Long at the gas station until your reason for being with him at the house in the woods and how you knew where that house was, in the first place. I didn't even know it was there." Troy leaned toward the young man, a kind expression on his face. "This relationship, you have with Mr. Long, needs explaining; the fact you would do what he asked of you, when obviously you knew something about it was wrong due to the fact the little girls were involved." Troy leaned back in his chair. "Now, you need a lawyer, before you begin let's call one."

"Russel," he called. "I need you to make a call to that lawyer over in Raytown, the one we...."

"Trust." Russel muttered under his breath. "Dang it, he's got the whole story and I doubted him," a smile tried to lighten Russel's tired face when he said, "Yes sir, I'll get right on it. He may come on like Andy Griffith but he ends up Perry Mason, everytime. I'll give him credit." He was dialing the phone, speaking to the secretary. "Yes, Ma'am, it's me and Chief of Police Troy Sanders request I speak with your boss." In a few minutes Russel hung up the phone. "He'll be here about one o'clock."

"Russel, did I hear you muttering to yourself?" Troy shook his head, "You are a dead man walking, I'm pulling rank. Now you go home and get some sleep. When you return I'll know you can handle what's coming down on us. It's coming with a vengeance, Russel, and I need you rested and all facilities working." Troy glanced over to Dawsey Koonce. "One last thing, I want you to make Dawsey, here, nice and comfortable in our safe room, away from prying eyes and any sound. He won't have to listen to Raymond Long bellowing like a mad bull. Like you, he's been up all night. We want him to have a good nap before his attorney arrives and it won't hurt none if he has a good warm shower, a change of clothing and the deep sleep of a man in search of freedom."

Russel glanced at the clock. Three hours. "I'll get right on it. Come with me, Mr. Koonce." Russel was showing a bit of respect to this fellow involved in Raymond Long's situation.

Dawsey got to his feet, swaying more with nervousness than fatigue. "Thank you," he said to Troy.

"Just down the hall, follow me." Russel opened the door to an eight by ten room that held the needs Dawsey Koonce could appreciate. A small wire shelf on the end wall held clean clothes labeled by size. Individual bags marked for men or women contained the toiletries that made them feel like a person again. Behind the wall the door opened against was a smaller room with sink, shower and commode. Under the open sink was another wired shelf with three white folded towel and three white wash cloths. Troy Sanders rearranged the empty space of the building and built the room when he came into office and it was there he showered the first of this morning after returning from delivering the samples of blood. Russel, genius that he was, had forgotten his extra uniform, which they kept in the small closet behind the desk in the office part of the Police station.

"There's no door," Dawsey said.

"No, what would we need with a door? But choose what you need from the clothes and when you've showered, just pull this down and there's your bed." Dawsey's eyes widened when the glimpse of the Murphy bed appeared and then Russel closed it back. "You won't want it in your way until you've showered. Now, if I were you, I'd get on it. Like me, you need sleep. You want to be able to communicate with your lawyer. Don't you?"

* * *

Down the road five little girls were gathering in the City Hall's room allowed by Mayor Stiles.

"This meeting will come to order, the Secret Investigative Club of the City of Perish."

Audi gave Nash a disconcerting stare. "I don't remember that being the name of our club."

"Do you like it? Does it sound more important than Secret Club?"

"I guess." Audi glanced at the others who seemed to already know about the renamed club.

"We have important business to discuss, following our trip to the woods," Nash said. "We must never eat or drink anything a stranger gives us. We did not know there was a problem with that juice the man brought."

"I actually liked you after I drank it," Audi replied.

"But something was wrong with it," Nash continued.

"Must have been," Audi agreed.

"Now, it seems Mr. Raymond Long is a person of questionable character." Nash glance at each girl. "We were supposed to meet with our Chief of Police this morning but Suz and Bentley couldn't make it, so I met with him."

"You have all the fun. I could have gone with you but you didn't ask me," Galanti said. "Why didn't you?"

Nash ignored the question. "Now, about the piece of material we saw in Mrs. Koonce car. Have any of you seen her driving around town, the last few days." They all shook their heads. "Then that's good. I told the Chief of

Police, Mr. Troy Sanders about it. I didn't see that other fellow, but I heard Mrs. Koonce's son was the other man that was with Mr. Raymond Long."

"Is he the one hurt our friend, Lily?" Suz asked.

"No, it appears that it was Mr. Raymond Long. The same one asked us to drink the juice we thought was orange juice."

"What are we here for?" Audi was tired and impatient. "We are out of school and I'm tired of this meeting."

Again, Nash ignored Audi. "I'm thinking we need to do surveillance on Mr. Long's establishment."

"The Funeral Home?" Suz exclaimed. "Count me out. I'm not going in there. It's probably dank and dark and dirty. I'm not going."

"Me neither." Audi was already getting up.

"Sit down," Nash ordered. "Do you want to be instrumental in saving the life of another little girl?" She stared hard at Audi. "Think about it. Who else cares about us? Who else could hide out and find more information to be sure that evil man is placed behind bars so he can never hurt another little girl."

"Did you sleep at all, last night, Nash?" Bentley was confused. "Our parents warned us to stay away from people like him and now you say we need to hide out in his building to listen for more information?" She was frowning. "You are asking us to go against our parents. They love us. They care."

"Yes, but they can't find information like we can. Who suspects a group of ten, twelve year olds?"

"If you get us in trouble, Nash, next meeting I will make a motion we dissolve this Secret Club that you try to run, except we won't let you. And don't look as though I hurt your feelings, you know its true."

"If you or anyone else decides to do it, then I have no control of your decision," Nash declared. "And you do hurt my feelings, Bentley. I have the concerns of everyone to deal with, you only have yourself."

"Let's vote," Bentley said. "All in favor of hiding out in the funeral home to learn more about Mr. Long."

"Not just Mr. Long," Nash corrected, "to all in favor to save our lives and those of other little girls our age."

"I'm not sure Mr. Long targeted us or anyone our age," Bentley offered, "But maybe we just got in his way. My problem is wondering what he was after when we got in his way."

Nash was counting hands. "Four in favor, how do you vote, Bentley? It doesn't matter. Majority rules."

* * *

When I was a child I spoke as a child, I understood as a child, I thought as a child; but when I became a man I put away childish things....

Chapter 13

The call came in to Perish's Volunteer Fire Department. It was a dash here and there as men who were willing to go the extra mile for another scrambled from whatever they were doing, arrived at the Fire Station that was connected to the back of City Hall, jumped on the ladders of the old engine pulling out onto the street and headed to the location received by phone by Jared Stiles, Mayor of Perish.

"Where we headed, Jared," Suz daddy hollered. He eyed the sky. "Storm comin."

"Don't really know but got the GPS going on my cell and have no idea if we will arrive in time to do much good but we're on our way. It's a country residence. There's a short cut for us to take."

Several pick-up trucks were following as they made the wild ride. Twenty miles away they saw the dark cloud of smoke rising to the sky. They arrive fifty minutes after leaving Perish to find a fire smoldering to the back of the house. Two other trucks from neighboring towns had arrived and were pouring water onto the roof. "We tried watering down the back as it seems that's where the fire started." The fire chief from Rayville rubbed his chin, warily sizing up the situation. "I'd bet my rubber boots its arson, my men found two old tin cans thrown into the tree line back there, and the lids weren't even on tight. They smell strongly of diesel in one and gasoline the other, enough in those five gallon containers to burn a house down, all right." He was leaning on an axe. "I already inhaled too much smoke, had to take a breather."

"Metal, huh?" Jared considered the information on the cans. "Not many have those anymore, maybe a few old timers. Where do you want us? There's a storm coming and the wind is picking up fast. That's not good." He was trying to give the man time to catch his breath, but his men were already on the scene, the truck driver, Suz's daddy had taken over and was waiting for instructions.

Rayville's chief was motioning his men to focus on a new hot spot of the roof near the front of the house where black flames were billowing to the sky. The fire was escalating, picked up by a switch in the wind. "You know whose house this is?" The Rayville Fire chief hollered to Jared a mere three feet away. Jared shook his head. "They used to live in your town, Jacob Long's parents." Now Jared was pointing the Perish truck driver to assist Rayville's men. "Fraley and Mary Long's home." The two were running toward the trucks. "We may have to put muscle into those fence posts. They're in the way of the trucks advancing. He took aim with his axe, Jared the other. The post splintered and fell to the ground. Together they drug them aside. Once more Rayville's chief was coughing, heaving for breath. After a few minutes, he shook his head sadly. "Mary and Fraley, they've put their life into this place. It's a show place, but…what…"

A loud boom sounded as the house roof collapsed where the flames were most intense. Flames were shooting out the windows. "Man, that means whoever set this fire intended for it to take the place down, but that's what arsonist do, isn't it? I'm calling my men back." As he said that, one of his men came running to where they were standing. "Jeff just got out of there, he said the place had gasoline soaking the carpets the beds, everything. We can't save it, it's too far gone."

"Get the men to safety."

His voice was grim. "That's what matters now." To Jared, he said, "That's Greenville's truck at the back. They arrived first. They said the back door was unlocked but it was my man went in to see what had been done in there." He was overcome by another fit of coughing, his eyes steaming tears, his arms flailing as he went down on the ground. A man with a medic container rushed to his side. "Dr. Goins," he said peeling away his gloves, hat and suit to drop down, Jared saw he was a young man in his thirties, perhaps. "Can you help me tear his suit away, we got to get to him, one way or another. "I got a temporary back up cylinder of oxygen in that bag, grab it and unfurl the line and we'll get it going. He's hurting. Then call nine-one-one."

Jared saw the man's eyes had rolled to the top of his eyelids, the lids wide open. If he was breathing at all his chest had quit moving. "He kept talking," he said. The words came involuntarily as if to explain what was happening as he followed instructions and made the call.

"Fred's a hospitable man, even if he's dying. If you're a praying man," the doctor said. "Pray."

Jared motioned for his men, pointing to the man on the ground as he dropped to his knees. The men came, removing their helmets to drop down beside him. It was a sight Jared would remember. Grimy, faces blackened by the fire, heads bowed, they prayed for the one down, the doctor's skill and for God to save him.

"Almighty God," Jared's voice rang out, to the crackle and intensity of the fire, and the sound of two trucks pulling around the house to safety. "Father of all, in the name of all we believe in, our trust is in you now as we come asking you to spare the life of this good man. Give the doctor the ability to do whatever is necessary, the skill, the knowledge, whatever it takes as we join together asking you to find favor in our prayer. This could happen to any one of us. You know our heart and our best intentions for others. W beg you, grant this day an ending of gladness and not sorrow. For we ask this in your Holy name. Amen."

The echo of amen, vibrated in the air.

The doctor was doing CPR. Another man had joined him to aid in whatever way needed. Sweat mingled with soot, the doctor's face changing with each downward push of his arm, his hands splayed across the man's chest. They saw he was getting tired but he wouldn't stop. It seemed an eternity, some of the men remaining on their knees while others stood a distance away not to crowd either.

The ambulance arrived, two medics jumped out, running toward the man on the ground. One took over for the doctor. "You got a weak heart beat, there, my friend," that one said to the doctor. "Good job."

"He's not out of the woods," Dr. Goin allowed the two truck drivers to aid him standing. He stretched his arms, twisting his neck to ease the cramped muscles of staying in one position too long. Turning to the others, "If he makes it, you men had a great part in bringing him to that point and I thank you," he said.

A voice in the group behind Jared's men said, "Dr. Goin's father is a minister. That young man has never lost his upbringing. He has a strong faith." The man began to clap. Rayville's Fire Chief was loaded onto the gurney to the sound of the men clapping their hands and they did not stop until the ambulance was out the drive headed to the hospital.

"They say life Is eternal," a big voice boomed from the crowd. "Yes, it is, but today reminds me we all have an eternity to face and I want to be in the right place. I'm thinking we all better be giving some thought to where we're going to spend it. Life goes on…eternity beckons. Where you goin to spend it? It's our decision and if the good Lord decides to take us and we don't have that question settled, then what we got to realize is this, it's too late. It could have been too late today. And it could have been any one of us. I want to spend eternity in Heaven."

* * *

They drove home at a slower pace than their mad scramble to reach the fire. "What'er you thinking, Jared?" Suz daddy glanced across where Jared sat staring out onto the roadside. A week previous there had been a flood, now the roadside ditch grass remained covered in mud but the water was gone.

"I was thinking what the man said about life being eternal, and yes, it is. Then he said but eternity is what we spend in heaven, which he meant after we die. Did you understand it that way?"

"Yeah, I guess that about sums it up." He sighed heavily. His hands were grimy on the steering wheel. "Like your prayer," Jared, "we don't know what will happen when we go out on these runs." He shook his head. "Most of our men are Christian. I say that, on the grounds we all attend church together. A few say they go elsewhere, I just pray they do know what salvation's about. We're a self contained group. Do you think it goes against a man's constitutional rights if we discuss this subject or, are we not allowed to ask if anyone needs to talk about it?"

"I truly don't know since we don't accept funding other than our own city revenue. We need help. Our equipment is getting old. We've worked hard to keep it functional, but the days coming when something fails. What then? We can't put our own men at risk."

"New equipment fails, Jared."

"Yes, but today it was a man's heart. I guess we are really concerned with the state of their heart, aren't we?"

* * *

"Did you hear?" Nash called Bentley. "I heard it on the six o'clock news. You need to listen. Your daddy might have something we need to know." She listened to Bentley's procrastinations. "Bentley Stiles, I'm calling a meeting tomorrow morning, early. We need to discuss this fire business. What if Raymond Long had a hand in this, too, it being Jacob Long's parent's home? Why, we can never be sure."

Bentley slammed the receiver to the house phone onto its cradle. Nash had her nerve asking her to spy on her own daddy. Wasn't that what it was? Spies listened. Wasn't that what Nash wanted her to do? Where was Nash's daddy? Was he there? And if he was, why wasn't Nash asking him. For two cents, Bentley thought, I would quit this Secret Investigative Club. But she had decided to write a book on their adventures, without the others knowing of course, and if she quit where would she get her material?

She shuddered. Her next chapter was to have been whatever they found in the Funeral Home. She couldn't quite grasp the title of that place. Why did people call it a home when they knew very well, whoever passed through those doors did not live there. They died and were passed through like a head of lettuce at the store. You placed it on the counter and it passed through to be paid for. That's all they were a head of lettuce. For some strange reason she felt unnerved and began to giggle, a nervous giggle that sounded more crying than laughing; a head of lettuce, where did that come from?

* * *

Audi Fields just knew Nash would be calling a meeting and she wasn't ready for this one. She was tired of Nash running the show. Nash Wethington. Her last name should have been Worthington. She felt she was worth more than the rest of them and maybe she was, but Audi had an uncommon bent not to follow Nash's lead. True, she was one of the younger ones. Why had Nash and Bentley allowed her to be part of their club? Then there was Suz. Suz Owens mother, Carol Ann, was friends to Elise Stiles, Bentley's mother but where did her own mother come in to this group? Sara worked in Greenville. She spent most of her days driving to and from the larger city that supplied her job and she had little time to visit around. It was a struggle for her mother to make the school functions for her own daughter.

Audi turned the television to her favorite station and tried to forget the club. If Nash expected her to do anything other than hide and listen at that funeral home, then she had another thought coming. "I'll quit, for sure," she whispered. "Who cares for us," Bentley had said. "Our parents care."

Maybe Nash's parents were too busy to care for her, no, that wasn't true, Julie Wethington was the one in charge the day that man came for all of them. They'd listened to him and sneaked out of the house. They could have died that day after he gave them the juice to drink. Now she knew, then she didn't. She had a dreadful feeling, the whole thing was not over yet but she decided, Julie Wethington was nicer than her daughter.

* * *

Galanti listened to her daddy telling her mother about the fire. "Seems it was Jacob Long's parent's home; what I could tell it was nice and the yard was one like you'd love to have, Ellie." Joshua Martin was scrubbing up; he had arrived home black with soot, stripping his clothes down to his underwear outside the door. "The yard had all these plants you would like. I didn't know what they were but every time I saw a man step on one, I could just hear you hollering, watch those big feet. It may be humorous now but I tell you when that man went down and the doctor worked so hard to keep him breathing, honey I thought, that could have been me. We get so involved fighting the fires we might not see what's coming our own way. He breathed in too much smoke. I've done that. The old lungs just won't take it. You should have heard Jared pray. The doc's daddy is a preacher, he said we should pray."

She heard her mother going in to the bathroom. Daddy left the door open but Momma would close it. "They think it was arson." She heard the rumble of her mother's words, probably getting on to her dad. "Oh, Hon, I told Galanti to stay put. She's on the sofa and I wanted to talk to you, so I left the door open. I'm in the shower, for heaven's sakes, not out there naked parading in front of our daughter."

Arson? Who would burn down someone's house? Why? Galanti wondered how was it, since Lily Delang died Perish had nothing but problems? Did they always have problems? No, no one had died. Now there were people kidnapped, give bad stuff to drink and a house burned. Was it the same everywhere? She felt scared for a moment. Growing up was supposed to be fun. Then she remembered the people Nash said had gone missing.

* * *

Nash made the call four times. The first was to Bentley. "Ask your dad if we can meet in the room."

* * *

"What do you mean, Jacob's parent's home burned to the ground?" Charlotte was stunned. Her mother was sitting listening and when she hung up the house phone her mother's words startled her.

"Jacob was here, Charlotte. When I awoke this morning, he was sitting at the breakfast table and poured a cup of coffee for me."

"You dreamed, Mother." She had found it difficult, rising from the bed, knowing there were a million things to do and for some reason her energy level was low and her mind set very forgiving of her body. "I can't handle this right now, Mother. I'm sure the activities we've been through these last days has your mind going a thousand different directions."

"He said to tell you Macie is fine and under the most dire of needs they had to move her. Jacob's parents received warning someone was coming after the family to teach Jacob a lesson." She sighed, sipping from her second cup of coffee. "Jacob made the coffee, Charlotte. He asked that you trust him. He says it is of the utmost importance we all trust each other right now."

Her mother sounded so sane and reliable, Charlotte sank into the opposite chair. "I wish I could believe you; especially that Macie is all right. But the doctor said she must stay in the hospital much longer and it would be only on his acceptance Macie could be moved. Don't you understand that?"

"Don't fret, dear. Jacob said they were nearby, not a lot of miles between as you suspected." Now, Elizabeth Granger leaned closer. "What do you mean Jacob's parents home burned. Are they homeless?"

"It appears they are." A frown creased her brow. "Where will they go, they are elderly, Mother."

"They could go to my house in the woods," Elizabeth offered.

Charlotte eyed her mother. "If someone has targeted them, in retaliation for something Jacob has done, in the woods, near no other living soul they would have no protection. They need a place that's safe."

Elizabeth replied, "I heard Raymond Long's rambling curse on the Long's and things he intended to do. He said he'd burn their house to the ground and take everything Jacob held dear."

"You didn't tell me or Troy that, Mother." Charlottes face showed strong emotion. "Why are you telling me now?"

"You think I'm crazy, Charlotte. You wouldn't believe me. Don't you realize I've heard everyone's comments? She's got dementia, she has Alzheimer's." Elizabeth's eyes became hooded behind the squint she wore, in remembering. "It's true; sometimes I know I'm losing it. The doctor gave me the prescription he said would slow it down. Do you know how it feels to be losing your memory, to not trust anyone for fear they will lock you up, away from all you hold dear?" She sighed as a tear dropped onto her hands folded in her lap. "Do you think any of it's easy?"

"I have moments things are clear as day, then I have times I can't think. It's like a fog rolls in, covers up everything I thought I knew. People's faces wear masks because I can't tell if I can trust them. I try to laugh those times but inside I'm crying, my soul is dying and I can't do a thing about it."

Charlotte left her chair, with pain dropping by her mother's knee. "You can never lose your soul, Mother. It is in God's hand. He will hold you there no matter what happens, no matter what people say, whether they understand or not, if I believe anything I know the faith you have always had will remain intact whether your body or mind…" She faltered, laying her head on her mother's lap. "I love you, Mother, I can't stand what's happening but I promise you, you won't be locked away from what you hold dear." She felt her mother take her hand in her own. She was her mother's little girl, again, needing the comfort and security of that wondrous love but she realized she had become the protector. Their roles in life were changing. How deep that love the years had fathomed, the breadth and depth few comprehend; the words from a poem evaded her mind and now she understood.

"Charlotte, promise me, If I reach a stage that I would harm you or anyone, then place me in a facility you have checked out where you trust the people who care for those less fortunate who cannot make decisions for their self. Promise me, Charlotte." Her hand tightened on Charlotte's. "Promise."

"Mother." Charlottes heart ached, her mother was trying to describe her despair, losing her mind wasn't easy. How she would miss that love they shared the day her mother no longer recognized or knew who she was. Right now her mother was concerned over Jacob's parent's home burning to the ground.

"Offer them the rooms downstairs, Charlotte. Do this for Jacob and his parents. Do it for me. I was not kind to Jacob or his family when you and he wed. Downstairs is as complete and finished as another house. I did it for you but you never came home, instead you married Jack. Then, when I was lost in my despair, your father built the house in the woods, our get away, a fantasy to relieve our minds of all the many strings of responsibility. There, we listened to music. There we planted seeds of a different life; we traveled to exotic places by films and garnered offerings one could view in the comfort of their chair. People thought we were gone on trips and we were but within a mile of this home. Strange? Only one who has had the advantage would understand and when someone was in need we gave as we could, in doing so we prayed God would forgive our many mistakes."

"I never blamed you, Mother, I made the decision to marry Jacob and when he divorced me, I married Jack, the kindest man I ever knew. He loved me beyond all of my shortcomings."

"I blamed myself," Elizabeth replied. "I was grateful Jack loved Lily." She sighed. "But when he died, Charlotte, the greatest gift you have ever given me was in coming home to live here, and I could see you and Lily every day. Now, perhaps you can understand the sadness I feel knowing my days of sanity are coming slowly to an end. I cannot dwell on the shortness of time but rather in the joy I will know until I can no longer understand what's lost." She squeezed Charlotte's hand again. "Call them, if you know where Jacob is, tell him to bring his parents here, we will shield them best we can and who knows, Charlotte, perhaps he will bring Macie and live here too. Could you handle that?"

Wiping her tears away, Charlotte got to her feet. "That is the strangest proposition I have ever heard, Mother. The world would think we are crazy."

"Everyone loves a love story, Charlotte. It would be a story of a different kind. Perhaps there are many looking for the same. Call Troy, he probably knows where Jacob is staying."

What had Jacob said when she was in the hospital? When the nurse called her Mrs. Long? Charlotte's mind went back to that time. "I didn't have the heart to tell her we are no longer married," he said. "Somehow, because we both are Macie's parent, they do not notice the different last names." And he had laughed, "Everyone wants a love story."

The white picket fence, the rambling roses and the mat by the door that said welcome, she thought. Had the years caused the dreams to fade from her existence, did her mind close door after door thinking she deserved nothing? But her child, her daughter, her heart cried out. Lily. Macie. She stared at her mother. Was she lucid? She appeared so. Elizabeth smiled. Charlotte's heart skipped a beat. This was her mother's dream, to correct wrongs before she was no longer able to perform the task.

"Mother, I must think," She didn't elaborate, the subject was too heavy and her mind full.

"Yes, dear, go think." Her mother's smile wore a sad wistfulness.

*   *   *

Troy's call came at the end of the day.

"Charlotte, a lawyer has met with Dawsey Koonce. He is turning evidence against Raymond Long."

"He will testify against Raymond? Are you certain? If Raymond gets to him that might change."

"I don't think it will. We've been through it all, thoroughly. It might save him going to prison."

"But he was an accomplish, Troy."

"He would have been if he'd meant to endanger the girls, Charlotte, but Dawsey Koonce thought Raymond Long had a love interest when he told him, rather demanded he go to the neighboring town for the date rape drug. He threatened to take the truck from Koonce. There's more than I can go into on the phone."

"I see." She wanted to ask him if he knew Jacob's whereabouts or if his parents were being taken care of, but she had much on her mind. She remained silent on the questions she needed answered.

"Charlotte, can you attend the indictment against Long and Koonce this Thursday?"

"Yes, I'll be there." She sighed, wishing she was ready to bring up Jacob but she wasn't.

* * *

Elise called early. "I guess you will be coming in for the arraignment, tomorrow." She became momentarily quiet. "Oh, for goodness sakes, Charlotte, have you heard the latest on Jacob's parents?"

"No, I've not talked to anyone this week, except Troy. We only discussed whether I was coming in."

"Charlotte, their bank accounts were stripped clean. They were in a reputable hotel but have been asked to leave. It's terrible, with their age to be made homeless and shamed before the public."

"Why are they made to feel ashamed? What did they do?"

"They have done nothing wrong; it's just being Jacob's parents. First their home burned to the ground and now this. I felt you needed to know."

"Who spreads such junk?" She felt sick to the stomach. "His parent's are good people. I would stake my life on the fact they have never done a day's wrong in their lives." Her mother had warned her, "More will happen to them, Charlotte. Mark my word, whether its Raymond Long hurts them or someone who was once their friend or neighbor, it is not over and they need and deserve refuge. Bring them here, Charlotte. It's the least we can do."

"They've been told to leave the hotel mid morning." Elise sighed. "I couldn't stand it if it were my parents." She talked a few more minutes and hung up. Charlotte placed the phone in its cradle.

Reaching for the cell she selected a number she held secret. "Yes, it's me. Find out where Fraley and Mary Long are staying. Draft a letter to them. We discussed the words, should life bring such a situation." She listened. "Yes, we need as near privacy as possible. Come in the back road and I'll let you in. Yes, call ahead and the garage door will open." Again she listened. "Prompt." I know them, they will not linger even if there is no plan. I will contact my person. Thank you for your help."

He arrived, legal counsel, until now, she considered a name from the past. "Yes, I will give you Jacob's lawyer's name. Together, I believe you can move this mountain. No, it doesn't matter the hurt from the past. It is the future matters. We have to learn to trust again."

* * *

Three minutes until ten o'clock, the attendant sit Fraley and Mary's luggage on the curb. The manager accompanied the elderly couple out of the building. She could not apologize enough. "I beg your forgiveness," she cried softly. "Never on my own, would I do this," a sob broke, "But the order came down from the main office. We are to set a plan in motion that you will wish you were not Jacob Long's parents."

Bewildered and broken Fraley stood beside Mary. "Stand strong, my love," he said, "God is not mock, I do not know who will He will send but we have prayed and someone is on the way."

"What if," she said, her heart breaking that they had come to this, "What if it is someone we least expect, a neighbor we would not have imagined, a church member we do not really know. Will our pride let us accept help?"

"It will be God in charge, Mary. We can do no less nor no more than to accept what he sends."

"It is a test of our faith, then, Fraley. I am not certain I am that strong. Do we walk down the street or do we wait. What has God said we are to do?" Weary, Mary wished to sink into the ground and not be seen. They stood beneath the hotel awning with its imprinted words home away from home and the lamp post with its brick surround that welcomed travelers. Mary leaned her body against the bricks.

"We wait," Fraley tried to smile. "Where else do we see a lamp post we might lean on?"

* * *

England Hornsby had flown in from Washington, D.C.'s own little suburb, Elizabethtown. Charlotte's call had seemed sketchy, as though she wished to withhold information but so dire was her need she had finally given it up. "I need your help, England. Years ago, you said if I ever need you. The time is now. My and Jack's daughter, Lily has died. The child I birthed with my first husband is in need of help, though it may not at this time appear so, she needs a benefactor other than her father who tore her from me those years ago. Can you help me?"

England Hornsby felt he owed his life to Charlotte and Jack Delang. They had taken him in, loved him, nursed him back to health when the world turned against him, his own family disowned him and his wife and children moved out of reach to another country, the one in which he was born. Yes, he would help Charlotte. He rented a car, drove from the airport in St. Louis and was now in her vicinity. She met him as planned.

"I have word," she said, after they had hugged and exclaimed how well each looked after the passing years, admittedly a brief time of smiling and lying to each other, she continued, "They are being evicted from their room at the hotel by ten o'clock. We need to be within viewing distance. How do you feel about that, England?" They sat in the rented car, staring down the street.

He reached across to pat her hand. "We are almost there, Charlotte. When we drive to the hotel entrance, the rest is up to you, whether you can persuade them to enter the car and if they believe you are there for their own good. Due to their age and the circumstance, Mr. Fraley and Mrs. Mary will wisely consider each step of deliverance. Age brings wisdom and worrisome circumstance makes people very cautious. It has been a decade since they have seen you. Can you rely on the past to make them trust you?"

"With Mary and Fraley," she replied, "there's no making them do anything, either they do or they don't." She gave him a weary smile. "They have based their life on God's goodness and mercy. We will see if this new situation has dimmed their faith."

At exactly ten o'clock, England stopped in front of the hotel's lamppost, sat reading the imprinted words on the hotel awning and waited for

Charlotte to do her magic. She got out of the car and opened the door to the back seat. "Mary. Fraley." She smiled. "I have come to take you home with me".

"Do you remember me?" She opened her arms to embrace Mary. She saw the tears that brimmed Mary's eyes and felt those boney hands upon her arms. Mary got into the car. "Fraley," Charlotte extended her hand. "You look a bit worn, Fraley."

"I never thought it would be you," he said, his voice a bit gruff as he held back emotions. He noted the man who was driving the car had opened his door, and was now putting their luggage into the trunk. Fraley reached for Mary's hand. They were each other's life line; God's mercy in person.

No words were needed. Peace settled into Fraley and Mary's heart as they held each other's hand. England and Charlotte spoke in soft voices about the roadside scenery, the miles they were covering and a nod finally to the elderly couple asleep in the back seat, her head on his shoulder. England winked and Charlotte smiled.

Elizabeth Granger was watching as the car drove up the lane. She thought she could see a couple in the back seat. She had not met this England Hornsby who was born in another country. Through a length of questions she derived there had been a scandal, a Washington scandal and Charlotte and Jack had become this England's best friend. "He lived a year with us, Mother, for he had nowhere else to go and now he is a trusted countryman. If I told you what he does for our Country you would be impressed."

* * *

Elizabeth went carefully down the stairs to the lower rooms that sparkled with the evening sunlight streaming through the walk out doors. The kitchenette was prepared, staples in the cabinets, the refrigerator filled, it was a nice little home for someone away from their own. She had planned it very well in those days when she thought Charlotte would bring Macie and live there, but Jacob had taken Macie and Charlotte had married Jack. God has his own timing, her mind whispered, perhaps he saved Charlotte's homecoming for such a time as this when she was most needed. He had allowed her to know Lily, though never Macie, but in the car now pulling up to the lower drive were the grandparents who loved Macie and shared her life.

She met them as they embarked from the car, perhaps a bit dazed she thought. "Mr. and Mrs. Long, welcome," she said and took each hand into her own. "Please, take time to be settled, feel free to explore and let your mind be at rest, you are very welcome here."

Charlotte watched from the short distance of the car as England unloaded the luggage. In time she would learn where the rest of their belongings were stored. Evidently for now, these pieces of luggage supplied their needs and what was missing would be met.

"How do you like that rocking chair, Fraley? Kind of like the one you used to sit in, huh? A bit large for Mary, but in the bedroom there's one her size. When you decide, if you want, we can move it in here." She smiled, content that the two were glancing around and seemed pleased with the surroundings. Two recliners faced the television, a leather sofa for napping, end tables by the chairs and an ottoman for tired feet. Afghans were folded to the arms of the recliners, the remotes easily seen, and the kitchen held their needs, plus snacks of fruit, favorite candies from the past and a few magazines she thought they would like and on the table two new Bibles, each with a name imprinted in small gold letters at the bottom.

"There's a bath," she said, pointing and two other bedrooms beside the larger, we thought you might like." Her heart was full as she said, "We will leave you now. If you need anything, there's an intercom, on the wall, there behind that lamp, just press the button and we will hear you. You will find a small laundry room behind the bath, but you have to go down the hall to gain entrance. It's kind of stuck conveniently between the other two bedrooms because it has a second bathroom within it."

Elizabeth turned toward the stairs. "Feel welcome to come up as you wish. Please, feel at home."

"I will leave you now," Charlotte said. "You may lock the door leading up the stairs if it gives you a feeling of security. This is your space. I hope it contains your needs. I am going now to try to find where Jacob is staying to let him know you are here. Perhaps if he were here you would feel more at ease?" Mary's eyes filled with tears. Fraley reached for Charlotte's hand, his grasp strong on her own told her more than words could have conveyed.

"I'll see if we can find him," she said. She and England left the two standing holding hands.

In the car, England asked, "Why the sad countenance? You have done all you can do."

"Sad," she whispered. "How many times do we forget, we must pass this way ourselves? One day."

> For now we see in a mirror dimly but then
> face to face. Now I know in part but then
> I shall know just as I am known.

Chapter 14

Troy Sanders saw the car pull into Headquarters. His plate was full and so was his bladder. He and Russel were having a difficult time. Dawsey Koonce had taken a liking to the safe room. "We were nice to you," he heard Russel expounding to Koonce, "letting you have a shower and a night's sleep before meeting with your attorney." Russel's heavy sigh reminded Troy of himself. Sometimes the job wasn't easy.

"But I'm scared to death of that man," Koonce said, as though he'd never done business with Long. "Could you turn me loose and let me stay with my Momma?"

"Let me remind you," Russel was saying, "you were an accomplice to a murder until proven guilty or not guilty by a court of law. We can't let an accomplice to murder go running around the country loose and certainly not Sand County. The people would have our heads," he heaved a deep breath again, and muttered, "not to mention our jobs. Now you settle down. We got work to do."

"Well, I need to see my momma; she always knows what to say to make me feel better"

"Let's see, your Momma's car is the one had that scrap of material in it that matched little Lily's dress. Am I correct? What you are saying to me is you feel your Momma should be here in jail with you?"

"No, sir," Koonce voice changed. "She would kill me if she had to stay here."

"Well, I'm thinking heavy on this, if you want us to bring your Momma in, we need to do some heavy footwork on that area of your suggestion and while we do, don't ask to go into the safe room again." Russel thought he finally held the key to Dawsey Koonce shutting up. "Now, I'll be in the outer office and your place as an accomplice to murder would be right there behind temporary bars of that cell."

"Temporary?" Koonce asked.

"That's the key word," Russel replied, "until proven guilty or not guilty."

"The lawyer said I supplied the weapon that was used, those rookies, but I told him Raymond Long threatened me. He said I needed to use better judgement and think things through if I wanted to live a longer life. But he did concede, wasn't that his word, conceded, that I was under duress." Dawsey Koonce cursed. "It was more than duress. He was going to take my truck away from me."

"How was it exactly you said you come into owner that truck?"

"I'd rather not say." Dawsey Koonce settled down on the concrete pad that was his bunk.

"I thought not," Russel muttered as Troy came into his space.

"You threatening the prisoner, Russel?" Troy's eyes held a glint of humor.

"Not him, maybe I'll hang myself today if he don't shut up."

"Take a peek out that window and tell me if you recognize that car parked on our lot."

Russel glanced out. "Well, I don't know who the car belongs to but Miss Charlotte is coming up the walk with some dapper dandy behind her. I bet that's a five hundred dollar suit or more."

"Charlotte? She wasn't scheduled to come in until tomorrow's arraignment."

"Guess schedules are meant to be broken, she's about to open the door to your very own inner sanctum."

"You watch too many episodes of Perry Mason," Troy replied, going to the outer office.

"Not lately," Russel denied. "We been busy ever since little Lily passed on."

"You need a wife to keep your mind occupied," Troy called back over his shoulder.

Russel heard him say, "Why, Charlotte, this is a pleasant surprise." Andy Griffith at his best. Russel wasn't certain if he wanted to listen or get on with work. Someone had to track down the name of that fellow over on the West end of the County that was letting his pigs tear up the neighbor's yard. Samuelson, he thought, all he had to go on was a plat book and the neighbors identifying description of where they both lived. "Can't have them pigs in the wife's Iris patch," the man said, "And if they get into her vegetable garden, well, she's going to shoot them. Done tore up the lawn. It's bad."

Rooted to the spot, Russel heard Miss Charlotte say, "Troy, this is England Hornsby. He has flown in from Washington, D.C. to help me. I'm going to try for shared custody with Macie, whether Jacob agrees or not, but right now, I figure if there's anyone knows where Jacob's staying, it would be you."

"Well now, Charlotte, you have come to the wrong person. I haven't seen Jacob and he didn't confide in me where he would be going."

"But the court has an Inditement against him," she replied, looking Troy in the eye, "Which means he can't leave the County and he has to check in with someone and we know that person is you. Seeing as how you and the Sheriff don't see eye to eye on much, I thought you were the one I'd start with and since I gave birth to Macie, I don't believe you would deny me a mother's rights."

Troy was staring at the floor. Caught between a rock and a hard place, Russel thought, because he had probably promised Jacob he wouldn't tell. Then there was Miss Charlotte what had helped him out on a number of occasions. How was old Andy going to handle this one?

"Maybe you need to ask his parents," Troy replied. "Wouldn't they know the whereabouts of their son?" Now he glanced up to study Charlotte. "I guess you know all about their situation?" She nodded."I'm sorry, Charlotte, I'm afraid I can't help you with this one." He turned toward the window, gazing toward Main Street. "Sure hope little Macie's doing all right under Dr. Cameron's supervision."

Russel wondered why in the world he would say that knowing Macie had been moved from the medical facility. But it must have been enough, his apology not being able to help. He heard Miss Charlotte say, "all right, Troy, I'll be going." The door was closing when she said, "See you tomorrow, Troy." Russel shook his head, how had the chief gotten out of this one?

"You gave up mighty easy on that one," England said as they got back into the car.

"No, I didn't," she grinned. "He didn't speak the words but he turned toward Main Street and mentioned Doctor Cameron. She's here, somewhere on Main Street and I'd say it's safe to bet Jacob's not far from her." She fastened her seat belt, "just drive slowly down Main and I'll watch for something to jump out and hit me between the eyes." England gave a chuckle and she went on guard.

"Rosie's Diner, Gulferson Shoe, Styles by Audra," she sighed. "Keep going. Mendolsohns Piano, Doctor's After Surgery Rehab." She thought a minute. "Stop. I think that's it. Doctors After Surgery Rehab. What better place to hide one's patient when you want to document her progress?"

"That doesn't take an ace scientist I suppose," England replied, "but why move her from the medical facility in the first place and put her in a place close to it? I don't get it."

"Her life was in danger. He had to move her somewhere and most folks would think out of town."

"You want me to go in, don't you?" He smiled. "Who am I the county inspector?"

She grinned, "You can do better than that but I don't think I want to know your plan. Just find out if they have…" She was at a loss for words. "I think, at this point, Macie needs supervised care around the clock."

"If they have the equipment in their facility to take care of someone who needs utmost care," he offered, "Maybe they would show me the equipment. Right?" He opened the car door. "Trust me."

She watched him enter the Rehab center. He was a very handsome man and he had overcome a lot of problems, rebuilt his life and was an employee of the government. With Jack in the picture, England had regained most of his business contacts and was making an honest living again. She wondered about his contact with the children? Had they forgiven his indiscretion? If not, would they ever?

She was beginning to worry when he came out. Smiling, he said, "They wanted to impress me. I put on my best Southern Charm and told them the truth, we have a family member who needs around the clock care, mostly we need a medically trained person would be in charge of her health's progress after surgery. They are proud of their facility and proud of their work. I'd say it's a good choice."

"You are stalling." She punched his shoulder. "Don't do this to me."

* * *

England Hornsby had arrived in Perish, invited by Charlotte to aid in her quest to find not only Macie but Jacob as well. England was comparable to the knight in armor, dashingly handsome, tall, a snappy dresser and seemed to always wear a smile. The truth was, he had suffered a broken heart when his wife left him taking their three kids with her. And where had she gone? Back to his Country, England. His mother with double citizenship had named him after his father's homeland. "We had good times there," he said she often reminded him. "So I named you England in respect to those memories your dad and I shared."

It had not been so with England, handsome as he was and vulnerable because of it, women fell by the wayside, in his path and once in his arms which was his undoing. That was when his wife left him.

"England, you've viewed the facility, I'm sure the Nurses fell at your feet, but what about it?"

"You really want to know, don't you?" He teased. Smiling and offering his cheek for her to kiss; she merely pat where he pointed and declared sovereignty. "Are you forgetting, you came to help me, not hinder nor make advances?"

"Advances?" Eyebrows artfully raised, he scowled. "Really, now, Charlotte, I passed that stage." Instantly he became serious. "It cost me. Yes, I realized women like a tall man that wears nice suits but that day, Carrie and I had a fight before I left for work. I thought I was getting even with her, when actually I was writing my own ticket to being alone, missing my children, the whole nine yard, Carrie, too."

"So, there's no reconciliation with Carrie?"

"She thinks there were other women. There were not. One discretion and I'm doomed. I did it. I own it and I'll work until death I suppose trying to right that wrong, but," he sighed, "Carrie won't take me back." Bitterness crept in for a second, "it was never worth it. Carrie shouldn't have had to face that."

"I'm sorry." Charlotte thought about the time he'd come to her and Jack, she thought Jack mostly but her husband said, "he needs to hear from you, as much as from me, it helps him try to understand Carrie's perspective." It turned out all he needed was a friend but she was sorry to hear Carrie wasn't bending. It was the children, she knew he missed them, too and he was thrown out of their life.

"Now for why I went in there. Let me ask you this, is Jacob a tall man, clean cut, has a small scar on the forehead?"

Charlotte's breath caught, "From surgery years ago after a baseball hit him, no doubt at a seventy mile rate of speed and Jacob was knocked to the ground and had surgery because of that hit. "You found him, didn't you?" A smile was his reward.

"Maybe. In one of the rooms there was a little girl that reminded me of the picture you sent once of Lily." He saw the moment's flicker of pain. "Loss is terrible, isn't it?" He considered his own, "Alive, my children are out of my reach." They sat there considering life's happenings. "What do we do now?"

She drew a small tablet from her purse. "It's my time. Let's see what I can produce." She penned a few words onto a sheet of the tablet, folded it into the envelope and got out of the car. "I'll be right back," she said. She had scrawled Jacob Long on the outside of the envelope. Inside, she had written. Jacob, if by chance you lost contact with your parents, Mary and Fraley are with me. We have set them in the downstairs apartment. They seemed glad to see us when we picked them up and once the hurt to their pride of being set out on the street from the hotel leaves their mind I think they will be all right, for Mary and Fraley do not waste time fretting over things as most of us do, they count their blessings instead and move on with life. We will see to their needs. Come to see them, when you can. Charlotte

She left the envelope laying on the counter top, the attendant was helping move a storage box from one corner of the room to the other. She waved upon leaving and gave them an encouraging smile.

* * *

That night Charlotte went to bed feeling her cup had run over as the Psalmist said. "The Lord is my shepherd," she whispered, "I shall not want, and Mary and Fraley shall not either." Her thoughts sped onward to her mother who seemed strangely happy knowing the two were downstairs. Making amends, Charlotte thought. How could a woman suffering dementia remember back to a time when she was not nice to a couple who had done her no harm but she blamed them for their son's behavior. Now, she hoped to correct any memory the Long's might have, but, Charlotte smiled. It would not be Mary and Fraley's way to harbor discontent or a grudge, no they would pray about it and go on.

Sleepy but not ready to rest, her mind still active, Charlotte began to say the words she and Jack had often quote together when there were trials in life. 'The Lord is my shepherd; I shall not want, He makes me to lie down in green pastures; He leads me beside still waters, He restores my soul. He leads me in the paths of righteousness for His names sake. Yes, though I walk through the valley of shadow of death I will fear no evil, for you are with me, your rod and staff comfort me. You prepare a table before me in the presence of my enemies, you anoint my head with oil; my cup runs over. Surely goodness and mercy shall follow me all the days of my life and I shall dwell in the house of the Lord."

Sleep claimed her body but her mind hurried forward. In dream, she saw Lily, running on a grassy knoll, balloons flying over head in a sky of brightest blue, the clouds fluffy white and her heart beat faster. She was running toward Lily when a small hand claimed her own and she looked down to find Macie running by her side. Lily turned, she was running toward them and when they met the two girls clung together. Jacob waved from the distance and there was a man walking with him. Charlotte leaned in close to see; it was Jack. He smiled, walking to Charlotte; he placed a kiss on her forehead.

"You fill my heart with gladness.' Charlotte smiled in sleep. "Thank you," she whispered.

* * *

It was late when Nash called Bentley, "We missed out on investigating Perish Funeral Home but there's the main one over at County Seat. We need to go there and tomorrow is the arraignment. What do you think?"

"I think you just as well quit thinking about going there, Nash. We're kids." Exasperation crept into her voice. "I'm tired, Nash and I'm getting scared we will get into something we can't handle. I overheard Daddy telling

Mother that Dawsey Koonce is a weird fellow and we know Raymond Long would hurt us if it helped him to get out of trouble."

"I'm calling a meeting in front of Acorn, tomorrow morning at eight o'clock. Be there."

"Don't tell me what to do, Nash. I don't think any of our parents would appreciate that."

"I'll see you in the morning. I've got to call the rest and wear your watch tomorrow."

"My watch?" Bentley heard the line go dead. "What does my watch have to do with anything?"

* * *

The day of arraignment arrived. Raymond's wife brought his clothes for the day. Russel studied the proceedings. White shirt, red tie, charcoal gray suit, not the austere black Raymond usually wore, the one that marked him as a mortician. He seemed to revel in the people thinking that, although he often was heard to sneer at his father who started the business, "I'll not touch that, no I'm not doing it."

The community assumed he had full power in the business and maybe he did. Oscar seemed neither to care his son's shenanigans nor how he spent his money. The man was absent from the community, more than he was in it. True, he built his home in the County Seat community but his business came from the surrounding area and Perish had lost a lot of people the last year. A lot.

Russel dissected the man's attire, not with a knife, but his mind. White shirt, authority, Russel would have chosen light blue; it was kind to a man's complexion. Red tie; oh, yes, that signified aggression, Raymond was a man to deal with. Or not. The gray suit defined a gentler person than one in black. Today he was a refined gentleman. Russel snorted. He hadn't studied how men dress, for nothing. Himself, he wore the uniform and was plain happy to wear it with honor and pride.

The wife sit primly in the outer office. Twenty years younger than Raymond Long, she was the second wife. Manicured, pedicured, adored and pampered, high maintenance. Yes, sir, high maintenance. Russel knew the first one. She was his age and had custody of their three kids, not like if she needed the legal papers, if Raymond Long ever visited his children, no one witnessed it, but Russel would bet today he probably asked her to bring them it for the Court room view for the honorable daddy.

Earlier, Russel overheard the conversation between Hightower, Raymond's lawyer and Raymond. "I suspect the room will be full," Raymond had said, "and the road on the way in, will be, too." He had taken a deep breath as if savoring the thoughts going through his mind. "They know which side their bread's buttered on."

Troy found Russel. "You wouldn't be listening in on our prisoner's conversations, would you?" He motioned his deputy to the front. "What's bothering you?"

Scratching his head, Russel said. "Tell me what I'm missing here. Raymond seems to think people will be lined up on the road, watchin' for his ride back to the court house square."

"I've never understood the workings of that man's mind," Troy replied. "Maybe he thinks himself some modern day robber. Like Robin Hood or you know a modern day hero."

"I'm waiting for more than that." Russel found what he was hearing unbelievable. "The things I heard him talking about sounded like they were coming from a wealthy old man. But Long, he was at his best trying to show me he cared for nothing or no one. I couldn't help wondering what the wife brought to his life."

Troy studied his deputy. "Through the years many stories have circulated about the Longs. One about Oscar seemed pretty cold to think a man would steal off dead bodies but Jacob seemed to want to clear that, though I have no idea why. He saw how his devotion was washed right out of the picture. Family ties mean nothing to Oscar and his descendants. Jacob got off to a rough start but I think the accident and now the health issue of his daughter has shown him there are real people out there who care."

"A lot of good that's going to do Jacob if Raymond gets control of his cousin's wealth, assuming he wins the case against him, which I don't see how he can. It's murder, Troy. Whether he intended to kill those little girls or not, he gave them a drug that could have, all to try to talk Elizabeth Granger into selling that piece of land in the woods no one knows or cares about?" Russel rubbed his chin in frustration. "What could possibly be important enough to go to all the trouble and run risk of being caught?"

Troy opened the desk drawer and brought out a piece of paper he'd received that morning from Charlotte's lawyer. Handing it over to Russel, he said, "England Hornsby explained with his position in Washington, D.C., working with various clients and extenuating claims that have to be settled in higher court this came across his desk. He had not once considered such probabilities would reside within our humble little town of the state of Missouri or that he would know those involved. Look at it carefully."

Puzzled, Russel was reading the article. "It seems surrounding states have discovered oil, but none has been recorded within a hundred mile radius of Perish, until last fall when Raymond Long asked for test, that amazingly enough were not on his property but on a hidden acreage few folks considered worth existing and few realized it was within Elizabeth Granger's holdings."

"You're saying Raymond had test run that proved he had discovered oil?"

"I didn't know that for a fact until receiving this report, but Raymond believed it enough to start the chain of events we're dealing with and the information passed through higher channels that involved England Hornsby. The man works with various government departments and one of them came into contact with the United States Bureau of Land Management. "

"Government agencies have developed laws that protect the rights of individual owners. Raymond accidently discovered run off into a drainage ditch that borders his property. There's a law of protection which regulates extraction by an individual other than the property owner where said oil originates. Raymond's intention to correct that was to purchase her land, but Mrs. Granger refused. He was taking advantage of her health issue, seeking her out, not intending for little Lily to be involved in the process but when she was with her grandmother Raymond had to deal with that problem."

"One thing led to another and things got out of hand," Russel concluded, "Little Lily died."

"Whether he panicked or not, we will never know, but then he became creative."

"A second visit to Elizabeth Granger who still did not realize the significance of his visit and it so happened this time the other little girls were with Mrs. Granger." Russel nodded. "I get the picture."

"Today's arraignment will be very interesting," Troy said. "It's nearly time to leave. I'm headed out to the car. At the appointed time, if you will bring out our prisoner, we will head toward the Court House."

"Troy," Russel went in to his usual fidget, signifying he was stressed about a situation he was not pleased with. "Uh, Troy, Chief, Raymond Long is demanding his wife ride with him."

"Now, Russel, you know that can't happen."

"Then," Russel muttered, his face turning red, "He insists if that cannot be arranged she has to ride with someone else."

"No one I know would be willing to take on that liability," Troy replied. "No." Staring at Russel he suddenly grasp the situation. "He wants her to ride with you?" Russel nodded, speechless. "It could be that would prevent another problem, if you know what I mean." He studied his deputy. "You decide."

Russel appeared ready to come unglued. "I don't like how this turned out. Long told me his wife would ride with me and I denied it, now you say she will….. you sure don't help out a fellow."

Shaking his head, Troy reached for his hat, stepped out the building and was closing the door when the Secret Investigative Club presented its self. "Ladies." He thought to proceed to the car but Nash stepped in front of him. "Can I help you, Ladies?"

"Sir," Nash began. "Is it against the law for minors to sit in on Mr. Long's arraignment?"

"I assume you are referring to the members of your club?"

"Yes, sir." Nash glanced at the girls now forming a semi-circle around the Chief of Police.

He scratched his head. Deciding it was all right to put the cap back on his head. "I don't suppose you would be breaking the law but you would have to have permission from your parents and a way to get there." He saw the look of disappointment registered on their faces. "Do you have permission?"

* * *

They watched the Chief of Police walk to his car. No, they didn't have permission because had they ask, it would not have been granted. The meeting in front of Acorn's had not produced a plan, though Audi was right, the Heavenly Supply truck parked on the street in front of Acorn seemed to be waiting for Mrs. Gracie Dalton to open her shop and receive whatever he was delivering.

"We could steal a ride with him," Suz offered. "I know he makes the rounds but when he opened that back door to his truck a while ago, I didn't see anything else in there to be delivered. Just big old empty boxes turned on their side. We could fit in those boxes."

"What if he didn't go back? What if he decided to go to Memphis or St. Louis? We'd be in trouble."

"Then let's hear your plan," Audi said. "I like Suz's." She grinned. "And I like that truck's advertisement. Look. Heavenly Supplys, right on Court House Square. We'll treat you right. Check us out."

"Do you know where the Heavenly Supply Store is located?" Bentley's eyes were on Nash. "You forgot, didn't you? Right across from the Court Room. Yeah, they'd see us get out for sure. Besides that, he won't come back tonight. He lives there."

It was at that moment, they saw Mrs. Gracie Dalton step out of her shop and wave to the Heavenly Supply driver. He waved back, getting out of the truck and went around to the side door, took out a box nearly as large as himself and struggled to the Acorn Shop. He disappeared behind tall bushes just before reaching the door.

They could hear his words, clearly. "I sure hate to tell you, Miss Gracie, but the favors you intend to hand out at your Anniversary Celebration this Saturday are not in, but will be today and I'll drop them off tonight." He sat the box just inside the door, and took a minute for a deep breath. "I remembered you said you needed a few days to work with these supplies so I came on over this morning but I'll be going back now. It's a big day, what with Mr. Raymond Long's arraignment. I hear a huge crowd will be on Court House Square."

"Well don't you hurry too fast," Miss Gracie replied. "And I'll see you tonight. I do need those supplys."

The side door was open. "Let's go," Nash commanded. "This is our only chance and you heard him say he will be back tonight. When he walks in front of those old bushes, hurry and get in. He won't see us."

They heard the side door slam shut. "I can't believe we made it," Galanti whispered. The driver side door slammed shut, they felt the truck backing out of the parking spot and then a blare of music came on. They were on their way to Court House Square.

* * *

Troy answered the cell phone vibrating in his shirt pocket. "Good morning, Sheriff." He listened. "Yes, Sir. We have the prisoner ready to deliver to Court House Square and if you feel it is your duty to walk him in, Yes, Sir, I guess I can go along with that." Sheriff Wade Bradford began his usual diatribe about his sworn duty to oversee the accused's rights until a jury found the person guilty or not guilty. "Yes, Sir, we are a minute away from departure. "Yes, Sir, if you want that is exactly what we'll do."

He closed the cell and stuck it back in his shirt pocket as a harried looking Russel brought Raymond Long to the Police car, opened the back door, and did the usual procedure of locking in a suspect.

"What's going on, Russel?" The door closed off Raymond Long hearing their conversation.

"Well, dang it Chief," He ran a hand through his hair, the ends already standing straight up from previous runs. "She started crying, the mascara running all over her face and her begging him to not leave her. Well, I won't tell you it got plumb embarrassing him ruffling her up all over, you know what I mean, her clinging to him and I was afraid maybe I'd missed seeing a gun in that big old purse of hers you had me to examine. What if he pulled it out shot me and escaped. It'd been my fault."

"But he didn't and here you are. Now, go get the woman. Put her in the back seat of the car and let's go. You've got the protection you need in the wire cage between the seats." Something else popped into his mind. "Here's another thing to think over on your drive. The Sheriff called. He says we are to pull in behind the Courthouse, unload Raymond Long into his car, and then we are to pull behind him and follow up to the Courthouse steps with our dangerous criminal. It is his sworn duty to deliver the suspect, not ours." Troy winked at Russel. "Maybe that'll get your mind off of your passenger. Knowing how you love the Sheriff's importance you might even smile."

Troy glanced around. He didn't see the Secret Investigative Club members. He sighed, relieved.

Raymond Long sit back against the stiff seat of the Police Car. There they were, his people, standing alongside the road, with hand printed signs. A few had bright red streaks accenting the words they'd written on cardboard.

"You were right," Troy muttered. "I suppose that's your fan club." He had a cold eye on the back seat passenger. "Can you read the words on those signs?" Raymond leaned forward, eager and pleased.

Thirty miles could have been a hundred to Troy on that day. He was thankful to reach the back lot of the Court House. The Sheriff was waiting. He opened the door to see Raymond Long, the six foot four male was not his usual arrogant self. Sheriff Wade Bradford eyed Troy Sanders with malice. "What have you done to our suspect?"

"I'm afraid it wasn't me, Sheriff. I'd say it was the writings on those signs the people along the way were holding."

"Were they threatening?" The Sheriff pulled himself into his authority stance.

"Let's just say not what Raymond Long was expecting."

I'll arrest every single one of them."

"I think not, Wade. Your name might appear there next time. I don't think you'd like to be associated with words like Baby Killer. Seducer of the Young. Killer of the innocent. Thief. Robber. Murderer."

* * *

Russel watched the process. He couldn't very well leave the suspect's wife alone in the Police Car. Somehow he wasn't seeing success written on Raymond Long's face. He seemed to have shrunk a few inches in height. He glanced across to see the wife's face registering the same disbelief. He had tried to get her in the back, Troy hadn't ordered the usual small spaced back seat of most cop cars. Perish surrounding area held a lot of long legged men and he got tired of cramming them in small space. When time came to purchase a new car he specified leg room. Now Raymond Long's wife looked lost in that back seat.

"Please," she cried. "let me sit up front with you. I won't do anything foolish. I promise."

Russel studied the woman. She was a mess and she was little and looked lost. "Leave your coat back there and that purse," he said. "Now I won't search you but if you got a weapon, tell me now."

She appeared dazed. "Where would I put it?"

Gentleman that he was, in spite of beginning drops of rain, he closed the door and went around to the driver's side. "Don't cry anymore." But when they arrived, she cried again. They hadn't said two words but she'd seen the signs.

"I'm afraid to go in there," she whimpered. "Not, without Raymond by my side."

"Well," Russel replied, matter of factly, "You wanted to come, so we're here, I'll walk you in and then, you are on your own."

"That's not fair." Huge tears spilled out of her eyes. The mascara began to run. "I have to ride back."

"Uh, uh, uh," Russel admonished, pointing at the tears. "You will be doing damage repair."

"But it's not fair."

"I bet Raymond's first wife didn't think a lot of things fair either. I knew her, you know."

"You don't know the story. She didn't appreciate him."

Russel held up a hand. "Don't tell me, I'm just a Perish City Law Officer. I don't need to hear your story."

"Then who does?" She seemed sincerely perplexed.

"A counselor, maybe, or a priest?" Russel scratched his head. "I can't help you on that. Now, get out of the car."

Stoney faces lined the sidewalk. Somehow all the fashion and flare of Raymond Long's second wife was lost on those cold bodies. They'd stood through a morning shower in order to hold their place along the sidewalk and now since the accused had arrived they'd go in and shiver under the Court House air conditioning. Respecting Russel's position, they lowered the signs, half-mast.

"This is his town," Mrs. Long complained. "Why have they turned on him?"

"Could be, it wasn't his town, after all," Russel replied. "Maybe he just thought it was."

"But," she whispered. "He paid a lot of people to keep quiet and he was really good to me."

"Uh, huh." Russel registered that remark for later. He'd hand it over to the Chief. Clearly this one's elevator didn't go all the way to the top. He parked at the back of the building as told and followed her around to the front of the building. She started to go up the steps and paused, turning to face him and extending her hand. "My name's Althea," she said. Russel nodded, trying to ignore her hand.

* * *

"They must have taken the back roads," He muttered taking his place by the Chief on the right side of the room, within fifteen feet of the Judge's station. He saw Troy's brows raise, questioning. "Our citizens. It appears half of Perish is sittin' out there, look at all Miss Charlotte's friends and there are three empty seats, I'd say Elise and Jared are savin' for Charlotte and England Hornsby. Wouldn't you?"

At that moment, Charlotte and the attorney from Washington arrived to take the empty seats. Russel smiled. Troy remained stoic, his arms crossed in front of his chest. He was wondering just how this would go; The Prosecuting Attorney having to bring charges against the one, who held his future in his hands, or so it was thought, but this was Atwell's opportunity to clear himself. If he handled this right, it wouldn't matter he was the representative for Raymond Long's suite for custody of Jacob, nor the fact he pressed charges against Jacob in the death of Lily.

Charlotte and Elizabeth swore to the fact Jacob had not been around little Lily and the night of Elizabeth's and the Investigative Club members rescue from the house in the woods, Elizabeth stated it was Raymond Long drew her out of the house on the night Lily died and Lily had merely followed her grandmother, the reason she was present at all. There was the fact the autopsy had revealed the drug in Lily with no one knowing how it got there until Elizabeth stated on the night Lily died Raymond had given Lily juice to drink just as he had her and the girls at the house in the woods.

Not any of that information had been brought to court yet, with the trial pending. Still, Raymond Long must think this case was already settled on the merits of who he was. Mr. Raymond Long. Then again, there could be a bit of fear building inside that bravo countenance that stared insolently out to other because of the people with their signs along the road into Maryville and Court House Square.

This was not your usual Court Case; this was turning into a Court fiasco. Troy took a deep breath, there was also the fact Jacob was under Charlotte's guardianship so to speak if one wanted to consider the Judge using the age old practice of friend to the court when he release Jacob to her. Almost, Troy wanted to sit down and put his head in his hands and wonder how it all really started. Would that have been years previous when Charlotte and Jacob were married? It was more than he could fathom. And where the heck was Jacob Long? At that moment Jacob slid into the seat next to Hornsby.

He heard the rustle of the court room attendees as the bailiff came from the back. "All rise." All eyes were on the Judge entering from his quarters. "The Court of Sand County in the city of Maryville, the State of Missouri is now in session. The Honorable Dred L. Collier presides."

The Judge took his seat, rapped twice with the gavel and said, "All be seated. Will legal Counsel come to the bench."

Troy noted Wade Bradford, Sand County's Sheriff glanced to A.T. Atwell. The Prosecuting Attorney gave a slight shake of the head. Raymond Long's attorney J.T. Hightower approached and stood by Atwell. He could hear the Judge speaking in a low voice. His eyes were penned on Atwell, "It seems we're on the other side of the fence, Atwell, are you all right with this?"

"I have no choice. I'm elected by the County and the safety afforded the citizens of Sand County."

"The man in question is your friend," the Judge offered. "You may recuse to avoid conflict of interest."

"I'm good."

"We will commence with the understanding should there be any disqualifying evidence presented concerning prejudice on your part,

Atwell, it is now I expect both parties to allow my discretion in presiding over this matter."

"Agreed." Atwell replied. The Judge looked to Hightower. Hightower paused, glancing at Raymond Long. "Agreed."

Now abides faith, hope, love, these three.

Chapter 15

"What now?" Bentley felt the adrenalin streaking through her body, her teeth were shaking. "I'm scared. I've never been in a Court Room before. What if they throw us out?"

"They won't. I've got a plan," Nash replied. "Just smile, all of you, not that birthday party smile, but the one where you try to be nice for your Momma when you don't feel like it…and follow me. I'll do the talking."

"Don't you always?" Audi muttered and Nash gave her a dirty glance. "I heard you. I will," Audi said.

Suz was miserable. "I really need to go to the bathroom. I might pee my pants."

"You are not a baby, Suz. Straighten up." Nash glanced ahead. "There's no time." They were entering the back door of the Court House. She had seen the officers going in and out. It was worth a try.

"You are fearless," Bentley said nervously.

"Stupid," Audi muttered. Bentley and Nash turned and gave her a withering look. Audi grinned.

"Hey, girls," A lady in a blue suit called to them. "You must be the Judge's granddaughter. Come this way, "Those your friends?" She asked Nash, as she led the way. "Stay in the Judge's chambers. Court is in session. There's just a door between this room and where he presides." She saw the look of surprise on Nash's face. "Oh, honey, there's a divider. You don't have to worry if the door springs open."

Before she left them in the Judges office, she waited while they surveyed the furnishings; A leather chair behind his desk, a leather couch in front of it and nothing but bookshelves behind, there was an interesting seal above the bookshelves that reached almost to the ceiling. As a group, each found their eyes rest on it. "That young ladies is a replica, similar to the great seal of the United States, but if you notice there's a single star beneath the Eagle's claws which depicts and represents the Supreme Court of the United States which our honorable Judge Dred L. Collier aspires too." She laughed. "He often says he's not sure he should have had the replica made but it's our secret and it keeps him forever true to the undeniable honor he feels to serve in such a place of responsibility to his fellow man and to the integrity of his Country."

"Now, I must leave you. Never open a drawer to the Judge's desk, nor think it would go unnoticed." She smiled. "Have a seat and the Judge will be with you within the hour. I'm so glad he informed me you would be coming in today."

"We are going to be in trouble," Audi murmured. "I hope your fancy talking can get us out of this, Nash."

"We must be quiet. I am going to open the door so we can hear. Don't anyone move, giggle or say a word." Nash moved to the door, opened it three fourths of the way and listened; with her finger to her lips, shushing them lest they speak, she nodded. They heard a man's voice.

"I contend it would be unlawful to deny freedom to a man who has not been proven guilty of such guiless accusations when he is and has always been a staunch pillar of the community, when his financial astuteness has funded many projects that have benefited the citizens of Sand County and most of all the surrounding communities that his business serves. I would ask this case be dropped for the fairness to the people of his community he desires to understand he is not guilty and based on his prior record of no offense to the law that he be allowed to walk out of this court room today with or without bail."

"Your Honor," A.T. Atwell countered. "Here, we have Mr. Raymond Long accused of being in the area where Lily Delang's lifeless body was found abandoned on a bench beside the road. A witness has come forward willing to testify that he saw Mr. Raymond Long there. Furthermore, he has been charged with giving a deadly substance to minors, the same substance as the chemical found present in Lily Delang and the young ladies he took to a previously unknown area, along with Mrs. Elizabeth Granger. That alone is grounds on which to deny bail and incarcerate the man but there's also the matter he has been charged with kidnapping those young ladies, a crime often demanding the death penalty, it is my belief Mr. Raymond Long must be held until a trial is set to prove either his innocence or his guilt."

Troy knew he stood taller hearing A.T. Atwell lay out facts and from the corner of his eye he saw Raymond Long rise as though air lift him from his chair and a gasp came from his lips that sounded around the court room. The crowd of people jumped to their feet. The rap of the Judge's gavel overreached their reaction until each person slipped back into his chair. Raymond Long looked on A.T. Atwell with a hatred that should have singed the hair off A.T.'s eyebrows. Pandemonium rose to be squelched by an austere Judge Dred L. Collier. "Silence, or I'll have the Court room cleared," he thundered.

Nash motioned they were to follow her. They paused just outside the door listening to the Judge's final words. It seemed Mr. Raymond Long was being held in Sheriff Wade Bradford's county jail and there was no set bail. The Court room crowd cheered as the girls slipped silently out the back door and found themselves standing beside Perish's own cop car. Nash tried the back seat door. It opened. "Get in," she hissed. "We know this one goes back to Perish. Get in and hunker down, as close together as we can get; that protective cage they use to haul transfer prisoners may keep him from seeing us. No noise. Don't even breathe. I don't care if your knees go numb or you pee the carpet. Just do it."

"There's a ladies cape, why don't we throw it over us?" Bentley asked, unfolding the cape and spreading it as Suz on the other end took hold and the cape went over their bodies.

"Good thing we ain't fat," Audi quipped and Nash pinched her on the arm as the sound of voices came near and Audi yelped.

"Shut up, Audi," Bentley hissed and they all drew together as the front doors opened one at a time.

* * *

The thirty miles was excruciating for the girls. Fear rend them silent but their knees were beginning to ache and their feet felt turned backwards and numb. They realized it was a woman sobbing in the passenger seat up front. They suspect it was not Chief of Police Troy Sanders driving. It had to be his deputy, the one people joked reminded them of Barney Fife. If that was true, he was a silent Fife. The most they heard out of him was a groan after each spurt of crying on the woman's part. What was the hardest to bear, her crying or his miserable groan, they wondered but their own feet hurt too much to care.

"All right," they heard the deputy say. "I'm going in to turn on the lights, then I'll come back for you. You must know where you are staying." His door slammed.

Nash waited, then opened the door behind the driver's seat. "Out." She commanded and they spilled out on legs that wouldn't stand at first but once the nerve endings received the brains command ran as fast as those limbs could carry them into the bushes. "Everyone go to my house. Now. I saw our parent's cars at the Court House. Its better we appear to have played hooky from school at my house than anywhere else. I'll take the blame."

An hour and a half later, Nash's parents returned to find five girls huddled together on the floor of their family room, fast asleep, their hands entwined and mostly covered by an old blanket from Nash's room.

"I guess if we hadn't all decided to have dinner together after the court session, we'd been here to feed them," Jared said. "They look kind of forlorn, don't they? Let's just call the other parents and let them sleep it off."

* * *

Troy Sanders drove past the Police Station. Russel had parked the car, turned off the inside lights and left the outside lights blazing. He was too tired to care. It had been an all-day session for him. When the others left he stayed to hear what his part in Raymond Long's stay in the Count Jail might entail. Then he and the Sheriff had a brief meeting, in which the Prosecuting Attorney stopped by, eyeing them as though he believed they were discussing him. "If you boys find my part in today's work faulty, then consider this, I am duly sworn to uphold the law that governs and protects each citizen of Sand County." Before they could reply he walked out the door and closed it firmly behind him.

At that point, neither the Sheriff nor Perish Chief of Police cared. "It's been a long day," Troy said.

"The irony is," Wade Bradford began, "That the Judge set Raymond Long's Court date on the same day Jacob Long is to come before him. Now what do you suspect that's all about?"

Troy's mind was full, the least not being his having to confront Jacob Long. Now he considered that conversation. "Well, Jacob, I knew you were nearby, that's why I didn't waste time looking for you. You indicated as much and I had enough sense to think you'd be near Macie. Now you know you are out of jail because the Judge put you in Charlotte's custody, so to speak if you were a child, which you're not and Friend of the Court's not regularly used on an adult," Troy scratched his head, "But now, our Judge is no dummy and if he should say to me, "Troy, where's Jacob?" I had better know or you will find yourself looking through bars, not because you're guilty, now, mind you, but because he left you in Charlotte's care. The thing is, you need to high tail it out there and make amends with Charlotte."

Jacob hung his head, staring at the ground. When he lift his eyes to Troy, he said, "Does it ever seem to you, the people who try keep getting kicked in the teeth and those who don't give a damn about anything progress?"

"You're thinking of Raymond, but today the Judge saw beyond Hightower's ploy to get Raymond off, and he did you a favor, so why don't you forget the comparison you just made, thank your lucky stars and do as I ask so I don't have to take you in? Because as I live and breathe, I'm bound to keep Dred Collier in my safe corner, you know what I mean? I need to be in good standing with our Judge and he's a fair man. I tell you, Jacob, this mess is fair wearing me out. You could use me for a friend too. So what're you going to do?"

Jacob glanced across the Court House Square. "I reckon I'll go with Charlotte, if she asks me."

Charlotte didn't mince words. "You ready to go, Jacob? Mother will be wondering when we're coming home."

Now, Troy wondered how that would go? Thrown together again, they could make it work and at least be friends for Macie's sake or swear off on that avenue and make life miserable for everyone. Their job now was to see Macie well, then they could explain the circumstance. He heaved a deep sigh, he was bone tired and he hadn't seen his girls in three days. Oh, yes, he looked in on them, but that was it.

* * *

At the Granger house, Charlotte drove into the garage, punched the button for the door to drop down and entered the house with Jacob behind her. "Does this seem a bit strange to you? Me coming here," He asked. "I don't like following you like a dog, but I know I need to… well, is it strange?"

"Not at all," she replied. "I left you a note, your parents are here. I think if you'd just claim the guest room again and in the morning go down and visit with them it might set their hearts at ease. I decided, seeing how frail they appeared standing on that street in front of that hotel that I could put aside my problems and focus on them. They're fine people and I remember their goodness. So you decide, are they worth forgetting our misery in order to see them through this season of losing their home and all those material items they collected through the years?"

He swallowed. "Thank you for bringing them here and closer to Macie. I had no way of doing it. My hands are tied." He was at a loss for words. "The facility let me sleep in a chair by Macie's bed. But I could tell they needed to kick me out and I had no place to go. Thank you."

"You're welcome," she said. "Now, it's been a long day. I don't know why I felt it was the thing to do to spend time with friends that were there as encouragement maybe for you as much as me, but I did and now its late and I'm beat. I just want to take a shower and go to bed. Good night, Jacob."

* * *

Two weeks passed. Jacob walked the short distance into town to see Macie every day. Each evening he gave the report of her progress to his parents and after the second day invited Charlotte down to hear the news as well. "They are weaning her from different pieces of equipment, no, no, she wasn't on life support, it's the convenience of the facility's skilled nurses, the hygiene she must endure for now, and the challenge to dismiss her knowing we are both aware of what to watch for, rejection of the kidney, blood clot, reaction to the meds she'll be taking the rest of her life. Those things." He paused to study Charlotte a moment. "How are you, Charlotte? Have you been well since giving Macie your kidney?"

Momentarily taken by surprise that he would ask, she replied, "yes, I'm doing well. No lifting or such, just taking it day by day and feeling the healing is taking place." His parents were listening to this exchange of words. "The question is, Mary. Fraley. How are you two adjusting?"

Fraley, as usual reached for Mary's hand. "We're doing well, too, Charlotte." Fraley's voice held a tinge of emotion to it these days. "We can't thank you enough, can we, Mother?"

Mary smiled. Her eyes on her son and the news they'd just heard. "We can't stay here forever, but having no place to go, for Charlotte to come for us was and is the answer to prayer." She reached for Charlotte's hand. "What can I do to help you, Charlotte?"

* * *

Climbing the stairs together, Charlotte asked, "You will bring Macie here, won't you?"

"If you are sure it's not too much on you and your mother."

"You have noticed, Mother's going through one of those quiet spells presently, but yes, I want you to bring Macie here. The question is, down stairs with your parents or up here with us?"

"Why don't we let Macie decide," he suggested and Charlotte nodded. "It can go either way."

* * *

Troy saw Charlotte's Navigator coming from the West as he entered the Headquarters' Drive. Surely Jacob was with her. The vehicle passed and he noted two people in it. Relieved he went inside. A wall-eyed Russel met him at the door. "Shh," finger to his lips he pointed toward the back rooms. "Uh, she's in there."

"Who's in there?" Troy's mind went into review, "I don't recall our having to pick up anyone today."

Russel swallowed hard. "It's," he paused for a moment to think. "What was her name? Althea? Yeah, that's right." Troy looked as blank as he felt. "You remember, Raymond Long's wife?"

"What in heaven's name is she doing here?"

"Well, you said she had to ride with me, so she did, then she rode back and when I'm locking up last night she says, "I don't have anywhere to stay." And I say, "Listen here, you're Mrs. Raymond Long, you got more wealth than ten of these Perish citizens put together." And she starts shaking her had, "No, I don't," she says. "If he was indicted for kidnapping and intent to kill, he told me to get my things together and clear out as he had no further need for me." Russel stared hard at his boss. "What was I to do with her?"

"You know better than to leave anyone here over night at the station without one of us being here."

"I was here, all right," Russel was shaking his head, about to come unglued. "I slept right there, my head on the desk. But she ain't my responsibility and I want to know what to do with her."

"Take her home."

"She has no home."

"For heaven's sake, Russel, she's Long's wife. Get her out of here."

"Well, Troy. Chief. She said he already warned her, if anything happened he wouldn't be available for a good while and she was not privy to anything in the home where they lived. It's his and she has nothing." His Chief of Police, the boss was staring at him as though he had two heads. "So, now what can you come up with, where should she stay and who can she trust from this point on?"

"You are asking me?" Troy looked as bewildered as his deputy looked innocent. "Russel, this is a Police Station, our headquarters, not Motel Six and you knew better, but knowing she got the better side of you I'll let it pass this one time. Now you get that woman out of our building and don't even tell me where you take her." Troy turned around and stomped across the lot to where Jared Stiles was entering City Hall.

"What's up, Chief?" Jared opened the door and held it for Troy to enter. "Well, I see we got more company. Charlotte just pulled in and Jacob's with her."

Jacob climbed out and joined them. "Troy, Jared." Jacob extended a hand. "I just came to tell you, I'll be staying out at Charlotte's. Seeing as she has custody of me," he grinned. "It's not easy to say, fellows but I tell you, Macie's looking so much better and all due to Charlotte, I can't fault her too much. Of course, if we live under the same roof awhile, different rooms of course, maybe different floors…only time will tell what comes of that; whether you come after one of us or not, Troy, for killing the other."

"Don't even say that." Troy scratched his head, "You know, more and more I'm finding the big things take care of themselves and it's the little ones kill you."

"You got a problem?" Jared's smile stretched across his face. "I could tell by the muttering as you walked over.

"No, Russel's got a problem. In summary, Raymond Long's wife has nowhere to go; no funds and she cannot live in the Police Station. I told Russel to take her somewhere. That is not my problem. It's his."

"Well," Jacob paused, thinking, "I can tell you it's no fun being homeless and with my own predicament I do know this, the women's shelter down on Vine's looking for someone to run it, I heard Raymond's wife used to be a secretary for one of his attorneys, that's where he found her." He grinned, "the grapevine's just ripe with news concerning Raymond right now and that means they're not talking about me." He turned toward Charlotte waiting in the Navigator. "Gotta go, they're bringing Macie out."

"There was a time," Jared said, "We were all close friends; it feels good seeing him come around."

* * *

The ambulance backed to the basement walk out and in a matter of minutes Macie was switched from the gurney to the bedroom just down the hall from Mary and Fraley's. Elizabeth had been silent for days but watching them bringing in the little girl her face wreathed in smiles and it was with warmth she reached across to squeeze Mary's hand.

"She walks each day, but for now with assistance," the ambulance attendant explained. "Dr. Cameron will be sending someone out the first few weeks to see how she's doing and that person can get her up on her feet tomorrow if you like. But she's good for going to the bathroom, just not alone, yet."

Macie was basking in her grandparent's attention. But Jacob could see she was confused as to why they were in this particular place and puzzled by Elizabeth's presence. He and Charlotte had sit down with Elizabeth to explain the circumstances, not to stress Macie they would let her become comfortable in new surroundings before introductions were made and yet, here was Elizabeth. Upstairs, Jacob heard the soft strain of music, Charlotte at the piano, something he realized she had always done when life demanded decisions. "Painter's paint," he had teased her in their married life, "and pianist play the piano, don't they?"

* * *

Thus, life began, Charlotte and her mother carrying on as before upstairs and down those stairs, Mary and Fraley with Jacob and Macie began a new season of healing. The insurance company had sent a representative to talk with them about the loss of their home and Doctor Cameron broke his rule and came to see Macie, beaming his pleasure in her healing. Going up the stairs he checked on Charlotte, encouraged there were still good people in the world and she was sterling in his book.

Charlotte's attorney met with Jacob before returning to Washington. "You have no choice in the matter, Sir," England Hornsby explained. "The child has a right to know her mother, but what's more significant is, Charlotte has the right to claim her child and I understand the two of you have agreed to move slowly lest the procedure be upsetting to Macie. I will arrange the documents."

"By any chance, are you acquainted with the attorney Charlotte hired for me?"

Hornsby grinned. "I thought you'd never ask. Yes, Demaree and I have faced each other in the Court room many times. He's a fine man. Should he ask my opinion, with your permission, I will be happy to comply." His expression became quite serious. "I wish you well in all endeavors."

* * *

A month passed; by now Macie took daily walks around the back drive with her father. Charlotte watched from the upstairs window, concealed by the voile drapes from Macie's view. How long, she wondered until Macie could be told of her existence? She did not press Jacob, but he knew her thoughts. Elizabeth, sprite soul that she was thrived seeing her granddaughter and Mary sensing no threat to the relationship she and Macie held, welcomed Elizabeth into their midst. When Macie asked how she should address the lady, Mary thought quickly and smiling replied, "Why not call her Gram."

The date for the trials was coming closer. Charlotte and Jacob spoke daily with the attorney's in Washington who would return on that day. Gossip in the neighborhood hinted Raymond Long's attorney was interrogating people in the community and it was feared they would be coerced into testifying falsely against Jacob Long but Hornsby said not to worry, he had investigated the Long's, their attorneys and numerous people whose names appeared on the list as witness for Long's defense. "We have our own," he said, confidently. "Our number one person will shock the socks off of Raymond Long."

* * *

The Secret Investigative Club came together. "We failed Lily," Nash said. "We were unable to tour the funeral home belonging to the Long family and we did not accomplish anything hiding out in the Judge's chambers, but perhaps we learned a few valuable lessons."

"What?" Audi asked. "If we failed how did we learn a lesson?"

"We tried." Nash replied. "Our single one piece of evidence will be used in the trial, according to our Chief of Police. He said Raymond Long had used Mrs. Koonce car that night and possibly did not hit Lily because no bones were broken, he thinks perhaps as Mr. Long carried Lily to lay her on that bench, her skirt caught on the rough spot of the car fender and he was never aware of it, so they will use that But the real cause has to be proven that he gave her the same drug he gave to all of us and it was too strong. The piece of material will be used as evidence he was there with her in Mrs. Koonce car."

"Bentley found that," Suz said, smiling at Bentley.

"Yes, she did," Nash agreed.

"But what did we learn?" Audi demanded. "I don't understand."

"How to stay friends," Nash said softly. "We didn't always agree, but I talked to my dad about how sometimes we didn't and he said the trick to being friends and staying friends is allowing each other to have an opinion and not disbanding because we don't agree…and we didn't."

"It's kind of like when my dad said that he, Mr. Lonnie and your dad's had been friends to Mr. Jacob when they were all young," Bentley explained to Audi, "and when he returned to Perish with health problems for a while they might not have supported him as they should have but when they realized they could have been the ones needing encouragement instead of Mr. Jacob Long, then they fell in line."

"Fell in line?" Audi repeated. "That means they agreed that they were his friend regardless?"

Nash smiled at Audi, her eyes bright with kindness. "Audi, you have come a long way."

"You, too," Audi grinned. "So are we disbanding? Are we going back to our real names? I kind of like my name now but I'm not sure it will look good on a wedding announcement when I grow up."

"Audi," Suz was laughing. "We do still play with dolls so that's a long ways off."

"Yeah? Well, that's the first you admitted it. "How about you, Galanti? Do you play with dolls?"

"Barbies," Galanti grinned, "in a big Barbie house, but I still take care of my doll baby's. You said its practice." Galanti, always more silent but keeping the record straight, asked, "So are we still a club?"

"I think we have to be," Nash replied. "There's a new kid living at Miss Charlottes. She may need a friend; besides that we may have to bear witness for each other when this trial comes up. My Dad says they may even call us to the stand because Mr. Raymond Long did take us and give us a drugged drink."

"I hope it has nothing to do with us stealing a ride home with Mr. Russel from the court house and that wet spot on the carpet." Suz blushed, admitting it. "I told you all I had to go to the bathroom and Nash said, no way." For a minute they all laughed, remembering. "And he never knew, did he?"

"There're more important parts to that trial than we'll understand," Nash continued. "I heard my Mom and Dad discussing it, Mr. Raymond Long was trying to buy Mrs. Granger's land because there's oil on it and that would make him rich…but my dad says if what Miss Charlotte says is true, they can't rush into believing it until they have their own tests made and as far as she's concerned the real threat was him taking us without our parents knowing and I got into big trouble over that for not telling."

"I'll say one thing, Nash," Audi admitted, "you do understand stuff better than me, but sometimes I don't like the way you put it. You did all right just now though. And I got in trouble, too."

"Let's dismiss and go to my house for ice cream." Bentley reached for Suz hand, on one side, Audi's on the other. "Join in, Nash. Bentley. Friends forever whether we are the Secret Investigative Club or not."

* * *

"Wonders will never cease," Troy shook his head at the news he'd received that day, and from Russel.

"What's that, Honey?" Gina slid down into the recliner opposite Troy's.

"Russel and Althea."

"Althea Long?"

"Soon to be Althea Pitts."

"What?" She leaned toward Troy. "When did this happen?"

"Seems Althea just thought she and Raymond were married. When he told her she couldn't return to the home while he waits trial, she sought out a lawyer in order to remover her personal things from the household, one thing led to another, the lawyer thought she would receive a wife's share of the property, therefore enabling her to enter the home even if to remove personal items, turns out it was a fake wedding. Raymond paid someone to appear as legally able to perform the ceremony. Well, she was disillusioned and then as the old saying goes, a woman scorned? Althea began to remember all the insane things Long put her through, his demands, his confessions about wrong doing threatening her if she told anyone, seems he had to get things off his mind. He told Althea and for some reason Althea kept a written record, dates, incidents, names of people. She has enough to put him away forever."

"She's smarter than you thought; still I can't imagine the two together. Russel and Althea?"

Troy smiled, "she says he makes her happy and Russel? Well, does a cat like milk?"

"Life is moving along in small town, U.S.A." Troy grinned. "And finally I am home for dinner."

"It's ready. Let's eat before you get a call." Standing, she reached for his hand. "I talked to Charlotte."

"How's that going?" He hadn't seen Jacob since the day Macie was transferred to Charlotte's home.

"She has yet to meet Macie, and it's breaking her heart. Jacob's not being mean; he just doesn't know how to present her mother to Macie. They are pretty intense trying to figure out what to do."

"What?" Troy's exclamation resound the room. "Time's enough. Charlotte and Macie deserve to know each other."

"I said the same. If they don't take matters into consideration, matters will take care of it, won't it?"

But the greatest of these is love....

Chapter 16

Discouraged, Charlotte sit down at the piano, from years of training and as pianist where needed, she went into a string of songs she kept in her head for times such as these. How were they ever going to bridge the act of telling Macie she was her mother and the one who gave a kidney for her health?

On and on, Charlotte played the piano, seeing the maze of black and white keys, her fingers on the ivories, her mind struggling to accept time had passed and it was past time that Macie knew who she was. Why had Gina asked if they'd met yet? Charlotte played the piano each afternoon, the songs depicting the inner struggles of her soul, the desire to meet her child and be acknowledged. Tonight the restless fever of her mind governed her fingers on the keys.

She longed to fold her arms around Macie's slight body, pull her into the confines of her own and place kisses on her child's head. Through the stress of her mind, she advanced to Spinning Song, her hands covering the keys, no need of music but a burning desire to see her child this night. What was she to do? The piano thundered, her fingers raced the keyboard, tears sprang to her eyes and ran down her cheeks, and she was becoming weary. She closed the piano lid over the keys, turned off the light and went to her bedroom. Slipping out of her slack and blouse, she slid between the sheets of the bed. She was sad, sad for Macie down stairs. Where was the comfort she sought? Yes, she lost Lily and Macie was not substitute but another daughter she had longed for. Would they risk Macie's health telling her? Jacob said Dr. Cameron stressed to leave the moment in God's hand and let him lead.

*   *   *

"Daddy," Macie was staring up at the dining room windows as she spoke. "There's a lady behind those curtains watching us walk." Jacob glanced up. "Daddy, why haven't I met her? Dr. Cameron said she was the lady gave me a kidney to help me get well. Daddy?" She saw he was in deep thought. "Daddy?"

"What, Baby?"

"Is she the one? The one who gave me a kidney? I asked Doctor Cameron, he said you would tell me. Can I meet her? I feel like I know her and that she likes me, but why would I think that?"

"She's a very nice lady, Macie." He paused and then added, "Yes, she's the one gave you a kidney."

"I thought so. She plays the piano so beautifully but the music is sad. Is she like my mother?"

"Yes."

"Did you love my mother?"

"Very much." Macie's face was a map of his own sadness as he glanced her way thinking I still do.

"Daddy, if she didn't die, where is she?" He was troubled for words. "If you loved her then, do you love her now?" Macie had not asked before. He must answer her truthfully.

"I didn't stop loving her, Macie, life happened and we couldn't stay together."

"Can I meet my mother? Is she so far away it's impossible, or if I pray, will it happen?"

"You pray, Macie. I pray over the matter every day."

"Daddy, I want to go in. After I get my shower, I need to go to bed and pray."

* * *

He listened at the foot of the stairs. It sounded like sobbing. At least the thundering music had stopped. He tiptoed up the stairs. He would tell her. Maybe tonight was the night. But he found Charlotte asleep, the pillow case damp. He understood why she was crying. Tomorrow, he would tell Macie the truth. He had leaned over to see if she was asleep, one hand across her body, balancing his own behind her as she lay in near fetal positon. Her hand closed on his. What was he to do? She would release his hand. She had to; his back was killing him in this position. He sank gently as possible, not to make her stir, his weight on the bed, easing down, conforming, his face rest on her shoulder, the tendrils of her hair brushed his cheek...and he remembered those wonderful days of their love and wondered what happened that they lost the gift of each other and from there he had taken Macie from her.

She did not loosen his hand, she seemed to back into the hollow of his body until they became spoons, nesting together, complete. He felt her sigh as he lay there listening to her breathe until his own eyes closed in blessed sleep. Somehow, he awakened in the darkest of night hour, coming fully awake to where he was and with the most nervous apprehension untangled his body from hers and the sheets. With trepidation he padded down the hall and quickly down the stairs where his innocent family slept.

For some inane reason he felt the need to walk the property. How many times in the last year had he silently viewed the proper lives of his friends, those people from the past he had known? How many nights had he yearned to return to the solemnity of those previous years when all was well? But it had not been well, and yet the problems had been but a jot or a wrinkle, never a failure, until his own actions closed in and he made mistake after mistake he had to live with and eventually face. Now, he would return to Charlottes' mother's home and allow his tired body to rest for the next day's ordeal.

* * *

Macie awakened to the bright of day. They had not disturbed her rest, the grandparents. Even now they were on their morning walk while the hour was cooler and did not sap their energy as quickly. She padded down the hall, glanced in to find her Daddy. She smiled, he seldom slept this late, something must have tired him exceedingly.

She prayed before sleeping last evening but something lingered in her mind; the playing of the piano by the woman upstairs. She had come to understand the house belonged to the elderly lady that visited Gramma Mary, but she was curious about the one who played the piano. She listened. All was quiet. Outside the birds might be stirring but here there was the calm of an eye before storm. She was tempted...but no, she should not invade one's privacy, still...she listened...it appeared no one was there.

She climbed the stairs, her feet dragging a bit as her heart picked up; she caught her breath and hand on the bannister rail she pulled herself up, one step at a time until there were no more and as she turned loose the rail and turned toward the big room, there it was….the piano.

Her fingers had moved each day, covering the sheet as though it were the keys, imagining this note went here and that one there, the rise and fall, the crescendo; and then yesterday there had been the thunderous music of one disturbed choosing to unleash the fury of the soul on the piano and she felt the woman's unrest for she had wondered many times of her own beginning and why the days were not always as those of her friends because something was missing.

Mesmerized, she studied the sheet music, the song. It was not familiar. Her hands traced silent across the ivory keys as she sat on the bench wide enough for two and then without thinking she pressed down one key and the next as the melody came, first soft, the tap of the keys pure, the rhythm increased with her sureness rising as she played the song, the sheet music waving, beckoning her on and on and Macie was lost in the glory of creation, the honor of others, the futility she sometimes experienced desiring to be better and then the soft and gentle wisdom of a higher power. Gramma Mary said she had the gift and your momma had it too, and Macie remembered those words wishing now at this moment her mother was there. She forgot she was in her white summer gown that touched the floor when she walked. Her hair lay soft on her shoulders and the joy of music and the piano lighted her face.

Charlotte awakened to the sound of the piano, at first hesitant, then exploring and now racing at times, other runs gentling down to a love between the pianist and the instrument and she found herself drawn to the room where the girl sat at the piano playing the piece she had written only yesterday. As though it was practiced a hundred times she sat beside her, their hands touching on occasion as they covered the notes page by page, feeling peace and contentment only they could know at this moment. Jacob had awakened and stood now mid-way on the stairs taking in the view of two in long white gowns, their hair touching shoulders and their face rapt with the melody time was allowing to happen beneath their fingers their motions fluid, a slight smile of satisfaction on each face and he prayed he had not let time overlap to erase that moment. His eyes lift to the photo on the mantel. It appeared Lily watched, also.

Finally in happy exhaustion they glanced at each other and came to a trickling halt. Smiling with the feeling of having done something good and exhilarating at times, now they stared at each other and as if it were an every day occurrence Charlotte hugged Macie to her body.

"Hello," Charlotte said, "Where did you learn to play the piano like that? Have you had lessons?"

"Yes," Macie replied. "Since I was little, four I think Grammama said, but she said I also have a gift, she called it a natural gift, I can hear a piece and then race to the piano and give a pretty good imitation of it."

"I'm impressed, you are very accomplished." Charlotte rose up from the bench and motioned for Macie to follow. They reseated, Charlotte in the Queen Anne's chair but Macie did not take the one opposite, instead she chose the sofa.

"Here," she explained, "I can see you better. Are you the lady who owns the house?"

"No, that would be my mother you have met. I believe she has told me you call her Gram."

"Is she well?" Macie's little habit of using her hands to help her speech went into play, "Nothing's wrong, sometimes she sits staring into space and I've seen another person do that."

"She suffered loss of one she loved," Charlotte explained, "Actually two she loved dearly have died."

Wistful, staring out the window, Misty said, barely audible, "I don't know if my mother died. Daddy says one day when I'm well he will tell me." She sighed. "But all these years I've asked, he hasn't." She met Charlotte's pained expression now, "Do you like me? I would hear you playing the piano every day and listen to see if I knew that piece, some I did. And I would feel that lady likes me and she only knows I'm here. She hasn't seen me. Had you?"

"No, since you have been here I have not seen you; I was trying to allow your family privacy. This is my mother's home; of course she will tell you it's mine, too." Charlotte laughed, reaching across to take Macie's hand, "much the same as I can say to you, this is your home, for we are here, aren't we?"

"Do you have a cell phone?" Mystified, Charlotte nodded. "Could you get it, please? I want a picture of us sitting at the piano to remember this day. It's one of the best days I've ever had." Charlotte reached behind a vase on the chair's side table and found her phone, handing it to Macie. "We'll do a selfie," Macie giggled, "come, sit by me, on my right side and then I'll send it to my phone so we can both have it."

"I have never accomplished those selfies as you call it." Charlotte glanced at the screen Macie held in front of her, "Well we look pretty good to have both slept in these gowns all night, don't we?"

"I heard the down stairs door, that means Grammamma and Pops are back from their walk, they'll be looking for me." She hugged Charlotte, lingering when she felt the response. "May I come back?"

"Any time you want."

Jacob had slipped past the bannister post into the hall concealed from where they sat at the piano. When Macie went down the stairs, he stepped to where Charlotte sat, her expression seemed dazed but happy. "We can tell her today."

"No, then she might not return to the piano or me, if we let her get used to me as we share the music perhaps that will be better."

"But it is what you've requested continually, now I'm saying yes."

"I didn't know what was best," Charlotte replied softly. "What we just experienced was wonderful."

"Yes, it was and the picture must be wonderful as well, the two of you looked so blessed."

"May I?" She offered him the cell phone. "Will you share?" She smiled. He sent the photo to the cheap little phone he was allowed to carry for his own health purposes. "And to Macie's?" She nodded.

Thus began the daily visits, Macie coming upstairs, the two playing endless hours of sheet music and those rare moments Macie showing her own compositions. "So you are going to be a composer?"

"What was your occupation in life before you moved back to live with your mother?"

"I was a nurse."

Macie got real quiet. "My Momma was a nurse," Grammama said. She went down stairs soon after those words that day.

* * *

On a particularly cloudy and rainy day when the sky loomed largely gray though the big picture window, Charlotte was cleaning a drawer to the large bureau that stood against the West wall of the room. "What's that?" Macie was drawn to the bright cover of the box.

"It's a word game."

"Can we try it?"

"We need more than two players to make it interesting."

"Will Daddy do?"

Charlotte laughed, "I suppose." Already Macie was scrambling down the stairs for Jacob.

"Oh, no, I'm no good at this." He pointed to his forehead. "Remember plate in the head?"

Little by little they were learning the intricacies of each other, what they liked and what they counted on. "It's time for your fancy lawyers return to Perish," Jacob said. Macie's head shot up.

"It's time for the trial? Daddy, if you have to go away, what about me?"

"You'll be with Pops and Grammamma." Jacob's glance held with Charlotte's. She shook her head mouthing no, not yet. "Besides, we're praying it all settles truthfully and I'm not accused of anything."

"We'll have to leave here, if they find a house, anyway." Macie's voice held disappointment, maybe a tinge of bitterness he questioned? But she was too young for that, still there was something else he couldn't read. And she was right, Mary and Fraley were looking for a home.

"What is it, Baby, what's bothering you?"

"I don't know," she whispered. "I feel it but I don't know what's wrong, just something's not right."

For a few minutes they played the game, but Macie's heart wasn't in it. "I don't feel good," she said. "I'm going downstairs."

"That breaks my heart," Jacob placed the lid back on the box. "This has to end, Charlotte. Let's talk about it."

"It can go either way, Jacob. I don't want to lose the trust we've built since the surgery. Macie could hate me because she can't remember when it happened, her leaving me for your parents and they have taken such good care of her...." Her words drifted off.

"For her sake, Charlotte, how far would you go to have your daughter's love?"

"Wherever I must," she replied. "And you?"

"The same. But we have to get this trial behind us and I have to know my funds are in my hands. I can't involve Macie in something as trivial or involved as all that."

* * *

The thunder rolled and lightening came up from the ground. It was the day of the trial. Jacob smiled sadly as he and Macie sat in the kitchenette sharing breakfast together. "How's that for a boiled egg?" Macie giggled. He had placed the boiled egg on the little stand only an eccentric like Elizabeth would have stuck into the kitchen supplies. The egg reminded Macie of Humpty Dumpty with the colored sharpies he had used.

"Is it safe to eat?" She asked.

"I am affronted," he said in his best English imitation. "Those are markers you could eat if you wished."

"Can I go to the trial, Daddy?"

"We've been through this conversation enough that you know you can't."

"I want to."

"Isn't there something else you want?" He smiled, placing his hand on hers. "Think on that."

"I do," she replied. "I think and I tell you but like everything else I don't think you listen."

* * *

With all the pomp and circumstance a small town could muster the trial would be Perish's exclamation to the world, bad things did happen in Small Town U.S.A, but it did not go unnoticed or unpunished.

A.T. Atwell went through the Court House from the front door, as did Troy Sanders, Chief of Police, Russel Pitts, his deputy, Mrs. Charlotte Delang, her lawyer Mr. England Hornsby, Mr. Jacob Long and his lawyer Clayton John Demaree and of course Sheriff Wade Bradford was already there strutting around the room as if he owned it. The Judge, Dred L. Collier entered through the back door, going immediately to his chambers until called. He had rather have been at an ice cream social with the community.

Of course there were other people present, but those were the important ones. Then, Raymond Long was ushered in from the County Jail in the presence of Wade Bradford's men. Full height, he'd been allowed to wear one of his expensive suits. He chose the light summer gray. Eight hundred dollars invested in that one, he'd let the fact slip. It would be printed into the articled for tomorrow's paper. Light blue shirt, Deputy Pitts noticed. The man had wised up. Those shoes shined so bright Raymond's face appeared in them when he bent forward.

It was when his ex-wife entered, Raymond seemed to want to spring forward, dip his pointed teeth into her jugular vein and watch her bleed to death. How would the people in the court room know? He stood up and shouted it. The baliff restrained him. Miss Althea didn't burst into tears. She held up a paper for him and everyone else to see. "You two-bit -----," he shouted, "it won't work." She smiled.

"It might," she declared, "Honey. It's from that book where you kept all your wrong doings. What was it you called it? Record of truth?" The people laughed but the Baliff shouted, "Quiet in the Court room or I will throw you all out." Miss Althea sat very prim and nodded. Raymond Long glared at everyone.

* * *

Nash didn't call the group, she sneaked in the back door as before and headed for the Judge's chambers. Problem was, he had not been called to the Courtroom, yet. "Young lady, to what do I owe this pleasure?" He pointed to the nearest chair and Nash slid onto the surface. "I take it you are my mysterious granddaughter?" He saw she was struggling. "That aside, what can I do for you?"

"Sir, I'm writing a book on our small town and I wanted to cover the trial. I'm sorry I did wrong."

"Not only that, you used your leadership skills to influence others," he said. "You need to think on that."

"I will." Before she could continue, the Baliff came to the door and nodded. The Judge straightened his body and stood tall.

"Stay and let us talk following the trial. Whatever you print, I want you to get it right." He closed the door firmly that led to the outer room. To the Baliff he said, "When I give signal, open that door a bit."

Nash sat there straining to hear. It seemed an eternity. Then, the door opened. She could hear.

It was the Judges voice. "In the Case, State against Jacob Long, A.T. Atwell prosecuting attorney, It is decided, No witness has proven Mr. Long's guilt in the death of Lily Jane Delang. In the case, Raymond Long versus Jacob Long for custody. Denied. In the case State versus Raymond Long the Court will continue tomorrow at ten o'clock." Judge Collier rose up, viewed the people of the court room once more, then turned and left by way of the door directly behind his station. Once in his private quarters he disrobed, changed from the white dress shirt to an open throat pullover, the dress slacks for a pair of jeans and joined Nash in the outer room.

"Young lady, what did you learn from what you heard?"

"That Mr. Long was not guilty of Lily Jane's death but we never thought he was and that Mr. Raymond Long has no right to take control of Mr. Jacob or his money, and that was never fair, anyway."

"Very astute," the Judge agreed turning his chair to study the great seal above the bookcase. "Your plans to be a journalist may change with age, you might consider being a lawyer and you could pursue your dream of writing on the side. Of course you would have to write under a pseudonym."

"Now," he asked, "how did you arrive here today as I understand you live thirty minutes or so away and do you plan to cover the continuation of Mr. Long's trial tomorrow?"

Nash was relieved she could answer truthfully. "My parent's allowed my being here and my mother drove me over. She did seem unsure if I should hear the evidence against Mr. Long as the gossip in our little town has built it considerably, and no one knows the truth. The Long family has been in control of lives in our area for years, it seems." Nash paused a minute thinking why her mother cared enough to be present for the trial. "I think both of my parents will be here tomorrow. Mr. Long taking us to that house in the woods along with Mrs. Granger upset them. I know they were very worried by the way they hugged me when Mr. Troy Sanders brought us back into town."

"You were very scared of Mr. Long?" The Judge was studying the girl. She was very open and honest.

"Well, not in the beginning because we didn't know what was happening at first. We were together. We knew him as a community person although I think he lives here; he has a business in Perish. When he offered us the drinks we thought nothing of it. No one ever said be careful of Mr. Raymond Long, so we drank them."

"And then what happened?"

"I can't remember how we arrived at the house in the woods, just that we were there because we were with Mrs. Granger in the beginning, and then he was very friendly saying it was a party atmosphere and we should all have more drinks and that strange looking man, Mrs. Koonce son, was the one who served us and I remember Mrs. Granger seemed a bit dazed as she said we should have cake but there wasn't any."

"You didn't really realize there was a problem until the Chief of Police showed up with Mrs. Granger's daughter?"

"Not really except Mr. Long had these papers he wanted Mrs. Granger to sign and she said, no, Raymond, my health being such as it is I don't do business without Charlotte present."

"Mrs. Granger is ill?"

"I don't know if she is ill or if losing Lily threw her into a state of sadness she can't overcome but she has been different she sometimes sits staring into space and doesn't say a word."

"I'm capable of doing that myself," the Judge chuckled. "But things escalated, I'm assuming, Mr. Raymond Long didn't like Mr. Sanders as Chief of Police interfering?"

"No, he did not. Next thing I know we are all loaded up and headed home. We slept because it was late and we'd had that last glass of juice just before Miss Charlotte and Mr. Sanders arrived."

"You have been most helpful, young lady but you do realize our conversation is off record and no one must hear what we've discussed. Now, tomorrow's events I leave your presence or absence to you and your parents. If I were you, I wouldn't bother." He smiled, "but then, this is what I do, I'm always here."

"Sir, how will I know the truth of tomorrow's hearing if I'm not here?"

"Good point," he said rising. "I'll see you to the door, Miss Nash. I'm glad we had this talk."

"Thank you sir," Nash left by way of the back door. The judge waved to her mother sitting in the car.

"Do you know him?" She asked her mother.

"I did once," her mother replied. "But that was a long time ago."

* * *

In the Court yard Square the news media were swarming around Jacob Long. "How does it feel to be cleared of all charges?"

"Right." He replied. Pushing through, Charlotte by his side, he was climbing into her Navigator when they asked. "Are you and Mrs. Delang together again?"

"We share a child," Jacob replied. "When my parent's home was burned to the ground by an arsonist, she brought them to her home because they are elderly and what happened was a trauma. I can't express my gratitude for that act of kindness, but no, we aren't together in the sense you imply, we are together on a higher level of respect and complete trust that we will do whatever necessary to care for the child we had when we were together."

"Was Mrs. Delang the one provided the kidney for your daughter? Why did you two divorce? Have you remarried, Mr. Long? Is there any love left between the two of you." The questions peppered the air.

Jacob's glance Charlotte's way said it all, who would have given them the information concerning Macie's surgery? "People talk," she said low enough no one else heard, "Some of Dr. Cameron's people." Jacob ended the media questions by shutting the door. Charlotte put the vehicle in gear and moved forward as the crowd stepped aside clearing the way. Hornsby and Demaree in Hornsby's rented car were behind them. "I told the guys to come out to the house; I hope that's all right."

"I feel so relieved I may collapse," Jacob admitted. "All these months I've been tied up in fear of what might happen knowing I had nothing to do with Lily's dying except to find her on that bench, and to wonder where the adult was hiding that was with her that night. I placed a kiss on that little girl's cheek and I wept that she wasn't breathing, my own heart not doing so well that hour grieving the loss and wondering why I felt it so deeply." The pictures on the mantel suddenly came into his mind. "She was mine, wasn't she Charlotte?"

Tears running down both their faces, Jacob turned to her and waited for her reply.

"Yes," she said. "She was yours." And in her mind she felt a moment's peace that his kiss had been on Lily's cheek. It did not erase the sorrow but it eased the sadness. "I'm glad you kissed her."

"I know it means nothing to you, Charlotte, and perhaps the timing is not right but what I said to the newspaper people is true I am most grateful and Charlotte, what I didn't say was, I never remarried because I never stopped loving you. I treated you worse than one would an enemy. I was messed up, I thought you were the enemy but it wasn't many days without you and I knew the wrong I had done and still I did not correct it."

Charlotte remained mute. "I'll finish by saying after the accident I was even more messed up but then I couldn't come to you. Out of the goodness of who you are, I couldn't have you taking me in for the reason of my being hurt, a mangled man with little capability trying to live for Macie's sake. I thought it was over. Gone." He stared out onto the roadside. "Coming home, I found there are other reasons to live life and be grateful. When you are reduced to the level of wandering roads, listening to people and unable to perform the simplest of tasks, that's when you begin to know what's really important." He glanced her way, but she was unbending, he couldn't imagine her thoughts. "You've heard the expression, Take time to smell the roses? All I had was time but I began to see what's important."

"We have to tell Macie, before she learns something from the news that sets her to thinking." Charlotte pressed the button for the garage door to lift. "It would destroy her that we didn't tell her first." She made no reference to Jacob's confiding. She had to find time to consider his long awaited apology. Perhaps it had no meaning now, he had not meant he loved her presently, he was explaining at that time when he felt loss. Pressing the remote, the garage door lowered and she hurried down the hall to let Hornsby and Demaree in the front door.

I know even as I am known......

Chapter 17

Business was the first order. "Tomorrow," Demaree said, "Hightower will pull out all the stops and go for the jugular." Hornsby nodded. "In review, Charlotte, if there's anything you feel would add to the validity of your Mother's case, with you her designated care giver, your lack of knowledge that there was oil on Granger land, or that your mother might have enlisted Raymond Long as he claims and promised him a share in the findings, now is the time to bring that evidence forward."

"Those are his words," Charlotte replied. "I don't recall in the months I've returned Mother ever mentioning Raymond Long. When others might make a remark as to his character, Mother only shook her head. He was never a close acquaintance, only someone she had known the family name. How could she have promised him anything when the fact he had looked into her private holdings has just come to light? I've seen every piece of her correspondence these last months. No, he is lying."

"Are there any witness to what your mother does with the hours of the day?"

"Like I've said, the neighbors keep a close watch on each other and a few talk every day. They will verify Mother stays home. She realized dementia was setting in and enlisted two people to keep watch against the day she might become harmful to herself, I don't think she has reached that stage yet. If anything, as time passes from Lily dying I think Mother is holding pretty good."

Their glance to Jacob brought him into the conversation. "If anything, since I've returned, Elizabeth seems better. She has taken an interest in Mother and Dad and they have become friends, but Macie…" he smiled, "She loves Macie and vice versa."

"Speaking of Macie," Charlotte smiled as Macie came up the stairs. "This is Jacob's daughter."

Macie did a slight curtsey, something she learned in dance class, and went to sit on the piano bench.

"Do you play the piano, Macie?" Hornsby ask. "Play for us."

"Only if she will," Macie replied, pointing to Charlotte and then scooting to one side of the bench.

"What shall we play?" Charlotte took her place and waited for Macie's decision.

"Why don't we play our composition and then perhaps Summer Place?"

Charlotte smiled and explained, "Macie is quite the composer and she has given each of us a special rendition, I suppose you'd say, to Summer Place…I think you'll visualize in your mind and of course understand what its all about." She turned to Macie. "Macie begins."

Jacob watched the play of emotion on Charlotte and Macie's face. They were naturals. The expression on each face of pure enjoyment could not be missed, nor the fact that Macie was a replica of Charlotte. He wondered if she had explained Macie was hers but Macie had not been told Charlotte was her mother. Still, there were moments he felt Macie knew, her very being accepted it was so, but Macie had not said. She was waiting to be told…subconsciously her heart made contact with Charlotte, their gestures were the same, their mind pattern and an overall goodness that could never have come from him were there but her conscious mind held back, was it because she had longed for her mother all these years but a tiny thread of doubt lingered, what if it were not true? She could not face the disappointment. How must they fix this problem? When?

The portrait was ready to pick up. Elise helped him, driving him to the artist in the near by town, leaving the cell phone pictures. He glanced to the fireplace mantel where Lily's photos sit. Would Charlotte feel a gladness or would she reject what he had done? Above the mantle, the simple framed likeness to a famous painter's garden paled in comparison to what the Artist was doing. He had measured, the one now hanging, twenty four by thirty six, and that was enough Angelo, the Artist said. "Give me two weeks."

"Beautiful," the attorney's were clapping hands. Macie was beaming and Charlotte's eyes were on him, accusing, he wondered or merely registering the grandeur of having Macie by her side. He didn't know. Macie slid from the bench, leaned to peck a kiss on Charlottes cheek and waved to her father as she left, going back down the stairs. "She is a delight," Hornsby declared. He knew, Jacob decided but Demaree did not.

"Yes, she is precious," Charlotte agreed. This time she did not look Jacob's way.

"We will be going," Hornsby said. "Demaree has a few tricks up his sleeve we need to go over."

*   *   *

Elise arrived shortly after they left. Charlotte let her in, "What a surprise, a good one, Come in. Come in."

"Jacob, there's something I need you to bring in from my car, if you don't mind."

"Oh, I'm curious," Charlotte said, taking Elise by the hand and leading her into the room. "So good to see you, my friend."

"I met the attorney's in their car on my way in. All is well?"

"We hope." Charlotte motioned, "Have a seat. Yes, today was a good day and tomorrow we trust will be also." They settled in as Jacob returned carrying a large cloth wrapped item. "Mercy, Jacob," she said, "That looks like a picture or something. What do you have." She smiled at Elise. "What have the two of you been up to?"

Elise was helping remove the cloth protector. The frame's back was to Charlotte. She was overwhelmed with curiosity. "I cannot imagine," she began to say as Jacob turned the painting for her viewing. Charlotte's eyes filled with tears. She arose to grip Elise arm. "Oh, my. Oh, Elise…."

"No, Charlotte, not me…Jacob did this."

Blinded by tears, Charlotte reached now for his hand. "I almost feel faint, it's so real. My heart is thumping inside my chest…." A fresh spurt of tears ran down her cheeks. "I am overwhelmed." She meant to back up to her chair but stumbled. Jacob caught her, her head came to rest on his shoulder and the sobs gentle and needing release poured out. "It's so real I could reach out and touch them."

Years of anguish, a child lost and another dying, disparaging words, the pain of living, it all came back to be dealt with. No one should go through life carrying such baggage when there were good things to come. They had ended those first years spent together under stressful situations and hateful accusations, but now it was time to put it all behind them. Finally, she backed away, wiped her eyes and sit down in the chair to stare at the painting. "Thank you."

Elise stooped to kiss Charlotte's cheek. "I'll leave you two alone." She heard Charlotte's protest. "No, really I must. Bentley has dance in about thirty minutes. I'm her chauffeur, you know." Elise let herself out. That's the kind of friend she was.

"It is beautiful, Jacob. How did you ever think to do this? How did it happen?"

"I think that was the very first time you and Macie met and played the piano together. Remember the cell phone picture?"

"You thought to add Lily in to the picture." Her voice broke again, always that moment of sadness came when she mentioned Lily.

"Lily's photos on the mantel, she was wearing white. You and Macie were still in your white night gowns that morning, almost identical, puffy sleeves, draw string neck…I was taken by the expressions on your face, pure and loving…I don't remember the song…only you two, and Lily on the mantel as though watching over both of you…." His voice trailed off. "Men don't cry…they say," he gave a feeble laugh wiping the tears away. "But they do. Men's hearts are moved, just as a woman's."

They sat in silence, staring at the painting.

"Jacob?" She turned to him. "You must have taken the picture from your phone to the artist, at least several weeks ago?"

"Yes, except I first had an enlargement made for his use."

"Jacob, that was before yesterday when I told you Lily was yours."

"Yes, but the day I was sitting on the stairs waiting for you and we were going to the first trial and you had hired Demaree…that day I sat there staring at the pictures of Lily on the mantel and I wondered. The two girls could have been twins. Due to health issues, Macie is small but I never met Lily, so I don't know." There was a catch in his voice…"or maybe I did, it is such a tangle of sadness…"

"Yes, it is." She agreed.

* * *

"My funds should be restored by the end of the week. There's a legal process, I'm told. Then, I will need to find myself a set of wheels. Do you want us to move out, Charlotte?"

Her breath caught in her chest. "I would be without Macie, again."

"We've imposed on you long enough. We need to do something. Now I can help the folks find things they need to move into their home."

"I'll help you, Jacob. I think we've come far enough that will be no problem."

He smiled. "I've grown attached to you again. I hope you don't mind. You are easy to lean on, Charlotte."

"You always said that."

"From now on, it's going to be the other way." Jacob turned hearing foot steps.

Macie stood on the top stair listening. "Are we moving?" She asked coming into the room. "I like it here." It was then her eyes rest on the painting. Charlotte felt frozen in time as she glanced at Jacob, evidently he felt the effect, too. Together they watched Macie examine the painting. "That's you, Miss Charlotte and that's me. Who is the other little girl and why do you have this huge painting of us?"

"I had it done, Macie, for Charlotte. The other little girl is Lily."

"Where is she? I want to meet her."

"She died," he said softly. "Sit here and let me explain something." Macie looked afraid. "It's all right." Jacob took her hand. "I have something to tell you and it is not easy to say that I've been wrong about many things. You have always had questions about your birth."

"And you always said some day you would explain everything." Macie glanced to Charlotte. "I want to know about my mother."

"Would you like Charlotte to be your mother?"

"Are you two getting married?" Macie's voice rose in surprise. "I like Charlotte. Could you love me, Miss Charlotte?"

"I already do," Charlotte replied.

"Well, this is not exactly what we had in mind," Jacob said, "It's harder than I imagined."

"Why?" Macie asked. "I said yes, because I said I like her and she said she loves me."

"But it may not be that easy," Charlotte cautioned. She was beginning to feel the unease, unsettled, in limbo, perhaps. "Tell her Jacob. Now it's up to Macie."

"Yes, I like the idea. I want a mother and I love Miss Charlotte, too."

"Macie, this is your mother; your real mother, the one who birthed you and gave you a kidney." Macie's eyes were wide, but Jacob was not certain her thoughts, surprise or rejection. "Do you understand? I took you away from Charlotte when you were a baby. She had nothing to do with all the years in between."

Macie was on her feet in an instant. "You could have come after me," she cried. "Why didn't you? "She was standing in front of Charlotte, at her knee. "I dreamed you'd come but you never did."

"Would you have had me to take you from your father, the daddy who loved you so much he kept you away from me all those years? It was wrong but he wanted you that desperately." A tear slipped down Charlotte's cheek. "I tried but the attorneys said he had the papers that proved I could never have you until the day he said I could. He was all you knew, was I to disrupt that?"

"Why did you do that?" Macie screamed at her father. "Why did you take me away from my mother?"

Jacob tried to pull her into his arms but she pushed him away and stood against the wall away from them both. She stood there for what seemed an eternity then turned and ran down the stairs.

"She hates us," Charlotte said. "Now, it will never work." Her head dropped. She stared at the floor.

"You're the one said you would have your daughter, she would remember the feel of your arms around her, she would know the sound of your heart. Are you taking back that one last thread of hope?"

* * *

They didn't hear from Macie that night. Jacob said she was locked in her room. "Mother said give her time. I guess that's all we have. Grammamma talked to her and Pops, too."

They went to the trial. The expectations they'd held for the outcome of Raymond Long's future held less meaning for them, now. Macie was all that was on their minds. It was complex. They did register the fact the woman thought to be his wife provided a book with enough incriminating evidence in Long's own handwriting to keep him in jail a life time. It seemed he had used the drug many times throughout the years. It was Raymond Long kept the family business going. Raymond provided people, though how he did it was yet to be determined other than by the use of the drugs, and Oscar stole from the corpse. They rode home in silence, a silence their friends felt as they left.

"We never know who lives next door to us, do we?" Jacob's random statement broke the ice. They could speak to each other again and their shared concern was Macie.

"Strange how so many things came together through this trial," Charlotte murmured. "It affected so many people, people from every day walks of life who want only to live well, to avoid hurt and be happy."

"What are we going to do, Charlotte?"

"I think Macie will determine that."

They heard the piano being played the minute they walked into the house and hurried to where Macie sat, her fingers nimble on the keys. She stopped, and glanced their way, her expression void.

"I've had a talk with Grammamma and Gram. Pops wouldn't say much. It's taken me awhile to think this through. They said they've been observing you two. You don't seem to hate each other; in fact you've been working together." She appeared dubious to that fact. "I don't know but there's one way out of this."

"What do you want, Macie," Jacob asked. "I'll do my best."

"You have to do better than that. I can't have you making a mess of our lives again."

"What is it?"

"You should know." Macie became the old soul of a child's wisdom. "I don't see how we can exist as we are now."

Charlotte knew a moment of fear, Macie's hurt could not forgive them. Silence hung heavy in the room. The child was measuring her words, she did not want to hurt them but she would speak out of her own disappointment and in that moment all three of their lives would change forever. "I'm nearly twelve years old and I've never had both of my parents." She cast her eyes on Jacob. "You took me away from my mother and I have not known her." Now her eyes were on Charlotte. "You did not come for me. I never understood why, I waited for you." Charlotte and Jacob felt Macie's misery wash over them as they stood before her. Charlotte uttered, "I tried." But there was no going back.

Macie shook her head. "I've decided there's only one thing you can do…it's up to the two of you, I never had a choice." Jacob reached for Charlotte's hand in reconciliation. "You have to get married. That's the only way."

"Well, that's incredible…" Jacob's relief was obvious, "but I think that's up to Charlotte." His hand tightened on hers. "What do you have to say, Charlotte?"

Relief flooded Charlotte, body and soul, except for Jacob's hand holding hers she felt the numbness leave but her knees buckled, the blood rushed to her face; her heart seemed ready to burst from her body. Had she heard this right? Her hands went to her face, amazed, emotion that had been bound so tight it coiled into nightmares that demanded unceasing prayer was being released, years of agony that had known only loss was replaced by gladness for each tomorrow as Macie sat studying her, waiting as though to say this is your one chance and I could take it off the table any minute. Her heart went back to regular rhythm and Charlotte felt reality sinking in; all those prayers, all those worries that she would never know her child and now here she sit only a few feet from her. She tried to speak and all that her mind could collect to try to say what her heart was feeling was, "I told you I would do anything to have my daughter." She opened her arms to Macie.

Jacob seemed as dumbstruck as she, but this was what they wanted, wasn't it? Still, her heart knew a woman's desire to have all things right, they had failed once and they could not fail again. "I will have to be courted and it will have to seem right for us to be married. Agreed?" She looked down at Macie and then to Jacob.

"I will not fail either of you, again." He reached for their hands. "I have never stopped loving your mother, Macie."

"I know," she replied.

"You knew?" Jacob's eyes were on his daughter. "How could you know?"

"By the way you looked when you said her name and your voice was quiet and strong like when you tell me you love me."

"This is our new beginning," he said, kissing the top of Macie's head, his eyes lingering on Charlotte.

The End

www.ingramcontent.com/pod-product-compliance
Lightning Source LLC
Chambersburg PA
CBHW030136100526
44591CB00009B/694